The Ultimate Teaching ESL Online Manual

Tools and techniques for successful TEFL classes online

By Andromeda Jones

Printed in the United Kingdom
www.bilinguanation.com

Publisher's Cataloguing-in-Publication data
Jones, Andromeda.
The Ultimate Teaching ESL Online Manual/ Andromeda Jones.

1. Teaching TEFL English. 2. Language Education

Contents

Introduction

Teaching ESL online is a well-paid and rewarding profession.

It isn't for everybody, though. In almost all cases you'll be working for yourself on a teaching platform such as iTalki or Verbling. This means that you'll be saying goodbye to a regular set of hours because clients will come and go — as will a fixed salary.

That said, after earning my living teaching online for the past couple of years, I wouldn't go back to an academy.

There are several good reasons for this.

The first is convenience. Time is money, and travelling between locations, if you teach businesses, or waiting for hours for your next class to start at the academy, means that you're not earning as much money as you could be.

With online teaching, clients come to you, meaning that you could potentially teach back-to-back classes all day if you have the stamina.

The second positive is the freedom that comes from working for yourself. In my experience in ESL, performance-related pay for academy teachers is rare. Your academy or school sets the going rate for your services (depending on location) and will pay you the same, regardless of your expertise.

With online ESL teaching, you are your own boss. You know your worth and what you can provide, and on most platforms, you decide your own rates and who you wish to teach.

Thirdly, and most importantly, are the students you meet online. I have always admired ESL teachers who teach kids, but it is not my thing. I have always found teaching children exhausting. In addition, I have not always had great experiences teaching at businesses either. The reason is that students in these type of classes invariably don't pay for their lessons. As such, some see their English classes as a way to escape their normal job and mess around for an hour or two rather than a place to learn something.

In my years of teaching online I have never met a disengaged student. Online students are professional people. They have opted to learn through internet classes because they don't have time for an academy. Nevertheless, they are ambitious and they want to improve themselves. Your online students will be paying for their own lessons. They will therefore be there to learn. They'll listen when you speak, complete their exercises with their full attention and do their homework.

At the end of the academic year you'll see a real difference in their language ability and they will appreciate your skill.

In short, teaching ESL online is great. It's better paid, attracts better students and is less demanding on your body than academy teaching.

'But,' you may be asking yourself, 'if teaching online has so many benefits, why aren't more ESL teachers doing it?'

Well, in truth, it's because it's not easy. There is a lot of competition on the platforms and, while top online teachers earn a good living, there are many more who struggle to find enough clients.

On language teaching platforms, students have pages of English teachers to choose from. With mediocre or even adequate classes, students will come to you for just one or two lessons before moving on to another teacher.

Teaching online is very different from teaching in the classroom. Top teachers employ techniques in their lessons which distinguish them from the crowd and build a loyal following of students who keep coming back to them for years.

These techniques take months to learn. This is why I wrote the Ultimate ESL Online Manual; to help new and experienced ESL teachers teach fantastic online classes from the moment they start.

This book aims to give you the tools to cut this learning curve from months to days, helping you to establish your reputation as a fantastic online ESL teacher right from the first lesson, whilst building a loyal client list who'll keep coming back for more.

Join me on this journey and let me show you how to become a fantastic ESL teacher.

How this book is designed

In part one of this book I will teach you the techniques you need establish yourself as a fantastic English teacher, online.

Next, we'll go into the absolutely best way to teach grammar and vocabulary: oral drills. Oral drills are a technique whereby the teacher feeds the student a statement carefully designed to get them to answer using a certain grammar point.

This technique is perfect for teaching online as it does not require books, power point presentations or any other paraphernalia; just the teacher and student orally practicing a piece of grammar.

Oral drills are also by far the most effective method for language learning because the student learns in the most natural way possible, through constant speaking and listening. This is exactly the way they acquired their native language as children (though now in a more controlled environment).

You can find more about oral drills in my first book The Ultimate Teaching ESL Manual, a step-by-step instruction manual to teach every grammar point in the English language.

The next part of the story is speaking activities. After a drill session you must provide freer speaking practice to allow your students to explore the grammar point for themselves.

For this reason, in part two you'll find speaking activities specifically designed for online teaching both for groups and for one-on-one online classes. These include roleplays, debates, stories and games.

In part three you'll learn the most effective way to teach questions and in part four you'll find over 45 picture and word worksheets which Manual owners can download from the book's site www.bilinguanation.com to display on the class's shared screen (the equivalent of an online whiteboard).

What this book is not for

Though The Ultimate Teaching ESL Online Manual will show you in detail how to use oral drills, it will not provide drills for every language point. You can find drills and/or speaking activities for all grammar points as well as 60 vocabulary sets, games, question practice and other resources in our original book The Ultimate ESL Teaching Manual.

This book encourages you to teach small groups of students (no more than four) so that everyone gets plenty of speaking practice. It is therefore not appropriate if you want to teach huge classes or MOOCs (Massive Open Online Courses).

Before we get started

When I wrote the original book, The Ultimate Teaching ESL Manual, I set out to provide a step-by-step guide for any native English speaker (with or without TEFL experience) to teach their language.

With The Ultimate Teaching ESL Online Manual, I extend that idea so that, together with its parent book, any native speaker now has the tools to teach the highest quality English classes online. There is a world of ESL teaching opportunities out there on the internet. Now you have the skills to access them.

Enjoy your new talent.

Part I

How to teach ESL online:

Ideas and techniques for creating the best lesson experience

1. Establishing yourself

There are a few ESL teachers who go it alone and attract students through their own website, but most online ESL teachers (including myself) work on platforms. This could be for a smaller company with just a few teachers who will teach a small pool of students, or for a huge teaching platform such as Verbling, iTalkie or Verbal Planet, where students can pick and choose their classes from thousands of different teachers.

Teaching on platforms has many advantages. Number one, you don't have to search for clients – there are thousands of students who already use these sites. Number two, you don't have to worry about getting paid, or arguing with the student about payment if they don't turn up. The platform will deal with this for you and automatically charge the student according to their rules.

The downside to this, of course, is that there a lot of teachers on these platforms already. And, a lot of teachers means a lot of competition.

Good teachers, however, are always booked up. They can often set their own prices as well, meaning that popular online teachers are, for the most part, far better paid than academy teachers.

But how do you stand out from the competition?

Making yourself heard above the crowd

Your introduction video

The first thing a platform will ask you to do is to film an introduction video. Your intro video is your sales pitch to potential students about why they should choose you. They are normally only one minute long. Potential students will view ten to fifteen videos before trying out a teacher and so a professional, engaging video is crucial to achieving that 'sale'.

How to film a good video

First we will look at the technical aspects of how to create a professional-looking video.

1. Use your smart phone. Unless you use one regularly, a video camera is not the best choice for this job. A smart phone will automatically focus on your face in 'selfie mode' to produce a clean image, whereas all the complicated settings on a video camera mean that a layperson will almost certainly film a lower quality video. If you use a smart phone, make sure that it's high-quality and can film at least 30 fps (frames per second).

2. Always film in good lighting. The best way to do this is to face a window. Place your phone in a small tripod, on a desk adjacent to a window. This is now your studio.

3. Make sure the background is not too busy. Clear away any clutter from behind you as the viewer will find it distracting.

4. Dress appropriately. Wear something professional but not boring (I would stay away from a suit). Don't wear patterned clothing because patterns often appear blurry on video which will distract people from what you're saying.

5. Frame the video to include your face and shoulders. Do not sit too close or too far away.

6. Be careful of echo. Have you ever watched a Youtube video when everything the vlogger says has a slight echo? Annoying, isn't it? A bad echo detracts from what you're saying. To avoid this, try filming in a carpeted room and place a blanket over the table you're using.

7. Use a teleprompter app on your mobile. You only have a minute to make an impression. You therefore must choose your words wisely. For this reason I recommend writing a short speech and using a teleprompter app on your mobile so that you can read the text. The app I use is Oretory. It's free and works great. Do not read the words like a robot — add passion and emphasis to what you're saying as presenters do on TV.

8. Look directly into the camera lens when speaking to your students. Be confident. Don't hunch your shoulders or put your hands on your face.

9. Keep looking into that camera lens and do not break eye contact. The lens on your phone is the little black dot at the top of your phone, not your phone's screen. It's very important to keep looking at that little black dot, even if you're using a teleprompter app and the words are appearing on the

screen. To achieve this, you must read the words out of the corner of your eye. This takes a little practice to get right but it is worth it and very important.

There are thousands of other teachers for that potential student to choose from. If you're not looking your student in the eye it doesn't look like you're interested in them. You must cease that moment, look at them directly and tell your student how you can help them.

Your pitch

Having said all this, great lighting and audio won't get you anywhere without a great pitch. You only have one minute to capture a student's attention, so what do you say?

Well, first of all let's look at what not to say.

Common mistakes to avoid when making your pitch

1. This may seem counter-intuitive, but don't spend half the video talking about your qualifications and experience. Students want to know what you can do for them, not about your life history. Furthermore, qualifications do not prove that you're a great teacher (the only way your student will know that for sure is by trying a class with you) they only prove that you have a lot of qualifications.

2. Don't talk about yourself in general. Lines like 'I like football' or 'I am passionate about travelling' should be removed. To be blunt, your students aren't interested in your hobbies. They only care about what you can do for them.

What to include in your pitch

So now you know what to avoid, let's move on to what you should say in your pitch.

1. Where you are from. Your accent matters and so you should always say where you're from in the first line of your pitch. If you're from a country with lots of accents (such as the UK) say that you're from the nearest well-known city.

2. Mention your CELTA or other well-known TEFL qualification so people know that you're qualified to teach English. Place any other qualifications in the description below.

3. Any other languages you speak or have experience in.

4. Your specialism. Some online teachers think that if they specialise in a particular part of English then they'll reduce the amount of students who'll sign up for classes. In fact the opposite is true. If you market yourself to everyone, you market yourself to no one and you'll attract fewer students.

5. Specialisms are important. They distinguish you from the crowd and justify a higher price for your work. So, if you're particularly good at teaching higher-levels, lower-levels, teens, the IELTS exam, the Cambridge exams or Japanese speakers then be sure to mention this in the first half of your pitch.

6. What you can do for your students. This is the most important part that so many online ESL teachers fail to mention. The reason a student has clicked onto your profile is that they want to know how you can help them improve their English. So what do you have to offer? Are you very good at correcting mistakes? Do you know how to teach English to people who speak their language? Can you unlock the mysteries of high-level grammar for them? Or will you patiently correct them as they embark on this new language that they have never studied before?

To illustrate what I mean, here is a sample pitch. I don't recommend that you copy it word for word but rather use it as inspiration for your own speech. You'll notice the second part of the pitch is all about what the teacher can do for their students.

Hi there my name is [insert name] and I am a CELTA qualified English teacher from Michigan USA. I have taught English in academies and businesses in Italy for the past 6 years and I speak fluent Italian.

I specialise in higher-level students; from intermediate to advanced level. I do this because I am passionate about grammar and the fine details of the English language. And so, if you're looking for a teacher to help you perfect your English who will a) correct your mistakes every time, b) tell you exactly why you're making these mistakes and c) practice with them until you eliminate them forever, then I am the perfect teacher for you.

So, if these are the sort of classes that interest you, then get in touch for your first lesson. See you soon.

Now you know how to create a great pitch, what equipment do you need to teach online?

What you need for your first lessons online

Technology

Apart from a computer, you'll need a good webcam (external ones are normally better than the webcam that comes with your laptop), headphones with a microphone and a fast internet connection.

If you are not teaching on a platform you must choose a communication program which has a shared screen feature whereby you can show your computer screen to the student. You'll need this feature when sharing pictures to teach vocabulary.

Free programs that offer this service include Skype and Google Hangouts.

Starter questions

The warmup activities that you use to start classroom-based lessons don't work online. The reason for this is that they are too complicated. At the beginning of a class, your student might have connection problems or they may not have tuned their ear into your accent yet. For this reason it is best to ease your student into a class by asking an interesting question to which they can give a detailed answer. For a full list of questions see chapter 8, Starters and Finishers.

Great homework resources

Students don't book classes with you just to learn grammar; they want a complete educational experience. This includes watching and listening to interesting videos and podcasts for homework and speaking about it in class. For this reason, the best online teachers spend a long time compiling a list of interesting homework material.

Setting podcasts or videos for homework also benefits you because a) you have a ready-made speaking activity for the next lesson and b) there is no marking. A complete list of the best homework resources can be found in chapter nine.

Visual materials

Whenever I have used visual materials in an online lesson, students have always been impressed. This leads me to believe that few online teachers use them, which I really don't understand. All teaching platforms have a shared screen facility where the teacher can show their students pictures from their computers.

A good library of visual materials will enable you to teach vocabulary that wouldn't be clear without a visual reference such as movements, landscapes and emotions.

They also enable you to teach difficult language points such as prepositions of place ('above', 'under', 'next to' and so on) which would be impossible without a reference picture.

As so few online teachers seem to take up this opportunity, by using visual materials, you will also distinguish yourself from the competition.

For this reason, this book provides over 25 pages of pictures which you can use for hundreds of activities. Other materials can of course be found on the internet and I encourage you to build up your own picture library.

A way to teach all grammar and vocabulary without textbooks

You can't use textbooks in an online class and so you need a way to teach all grammar and vocabulary points without them. The best way to do this is through oral drills and speaking activities. For more on oral drills, go to chapter three: How to Teach Grammar and Vocabulary with Oral Drills.

Now that you have a great introduction video and a rich library of resources, let's move on to chapter two to discover the most effective way to teach ESL classes online.

2. How to teach fantastic ESL classes online

How teaching online is different from teaching offline

If you've normally taught group lessons in academies or schools, you're going to find online teaching very different.

The main difference is that most classes online are with individual students rather than a class. This is a significant because in a classroom the teacher sets students work to do in pairs. This means that for classroom lessons, the teacher will take on more of a supervisor role as students conduct speaking activities with their partner. In addition, because the teacher has to explain the task to 10 people rather than one, activities last longer.

In an online class, speaking activities happen between the student and teacher, meaning that they require more effort from the teacher and are much shorter.

For this reason, your lessons should be shorter online and kept to a maximum of one hour. You should also plan for your speaking activities to take half the time.

How teach a fantastic class and keep students coming back

So you have posted a professional, engaging introduction video and attracted your first students for a trial class. Now, how do you turn these one-class students into regular clients?

Your first class with a new student

First of all, introduce yourself. Keep it short and immediately turn the question back to the student. For example, 'Hi, I'm Kevin. I'm an English teacher from Ireland. What about you?'

Ask your student to explain as much about themselves as possible. Information to obtain includes, their name, where they live, what they do for a living or (if they are a student) what they are studying.

Beyond personal details, three other crucial questions to ask are:

1. Why are you studying English?
2. When do you need to use English in your everyday life?
3. Is there anything you would like to practice today? Do they have an interview coming up, or a presentation, or an exam?

Next, I usually explain that I need to get an idea of the student's level and so I will ask a question and ask the student to give the most complete question they can. My go-to question for this is:

'Tell me about a book or film that has influenced your life.'

I use this question because everyone has at least one book or film that they love and there is lots of scope for speaking. They can talk about the story, where they were in their lives when they read the book or saw the movie and how it affected them. While they are speaking, correct the student on their mistakes and write down any consistent grammatical errors as something to practice this class.

This speaking practice normally lasts for around 10 minutes. You student will be satisfied because they have had the chance to practice speaking right from the start and you will have gained valuable insight into their linguistic strengths and weaknesses.

It's at this point where I explain the structure of my lessons. This is 50% speaking practice and 50% grammar or vocabulary instruction. I have this structure because this is honestly the best way to retain students.

I have had many new students say to me that they just want to practice speaking. I understand their reasoning; they want to speak to improve their fluency. However, without proper grammar instruction, these students will never understand *why* they are making the mistakes that they do and will therefore never learn to speak accurately. Over time, these students, who just want to chat, will realise that they are not improving and drop out.

For this reason I, and the most successful online teachers I know, create a program for the student to follow. In each lesson the student reviews what they learnt in the previous lesson and then learns something new.

At the end of each lesson you should propose the topic of the next lesson and ask if they agree. If the student prefers to study something else, create a class on the grammar or vocabulary point they want to study next. The important thing is that the student knows that they are on a trajectory and they can be confident that they will learn something new every lesson. If you stick to a program, your students will be less likely to leave you for another teacher. This is because if they switch teachers halfway through your program they know that they may have to go through much of the grammar they learned with you, again, with another teacher. If they stick with you, however, they are always guaranteed to learn something new.

So now you know how to retain new students, what is the structure of a class with regular students?

How to teach regular students

Beginning a lesson

Begin your lesson with an easy speaking practice to get your students used to speaking English again. Ask them to tell you about the podcast or video they listened to for homework. This is often a student's favourite part of the lesson – they learned something new (and hopefully interesting) with the homework activity and now they'll want to tell you about it. You should ask them a few questions about the subject and what new vocabulary they have discovered. Spend at least 10 minutes on this task.

If they are a new student or they didn't do their homework, ask them an open question such as, 'tell me about a place you have visited which has impressed you.' You can find a list of these questions in the Starters and Finishers chapter.

Review what they learned the previous lesson

At the beginning of each lesson spend five to 10 minutes going through what you did last lesson and test your students on their knowledge. If they do well, then move on. If they don't do well, spend more time on it.

Teach your students something new

This is the most important part of the class. Teach your students the grammar or vocabulary point you agreed upon last lesson.

Eliciting

As you probably know, a language teacher does not (and cannot) plant information in a student's brain. A language teacher facilitates a student's learning while they decipher how a language point works *for themselves*. The most effective way to do this is through eliciting.

Eliciting is a technique whereby the teacher, instead of trying to explain the point, extracts information from students through questioning techniques.

For example, if you're teaching the present perfect tense, you would write an example sentence such as 'she has eaten an apple today.'

Instead of giving information and hoping they understand, it is much more effective for your students to teach themselves by answering your questions. Questions could be:

- 'what is the tense?'
- 'what is the difference between "she has eaten an apple" and "she ate an apple?"'
- 'What is the negative of this sentence?'
- And finally, 'give me another sentence in this tense.'

Eliciting, rather than explaining, also has another benefit; you'll end up speaking less. A day of back-to-back classes is hard work and you must use techniques to save your voice whenever you can. It is much more energy efficient to ask some leading questions, getting the student to explain the language point to you.

Practice the new point with drills

After a student understands a new language point, you have to find a way for them to practice it. The most effective way is through oral drills. To find out more about oral drills, see chapter three.

Freer speaking practice

Now you must find a way for your student to practice the grammar or vocabulary point freely. This could be with role play exercises, such as the ones you'll find at the back of this book, or by asking an open question. For example, to practice the simple past, I often ask a student to recount their last big holiday or, if they like history, to tell me about a famous historical figure or event. For more speaking practice ideas, go to chapter four.

The last five minutes: Answering questions, setting homework, talking about the next lesson

In the final five minutes of the class, I ask if the student has any questions about the language point you practiced. I then set some homework, which is always to listen to a podcast or to watch an informative video. This type of homework serves a dual purpose. It first provides valuable comprehension practice, and second, a ten minute speaking activity for the following lesson.

I also set some writing homework. This is normally to write 10 sentences using the grammar or vocabulary we studied. Students like this homework because it clarifies the point in their minds. This type of homework normally takes only five minutes to correct.

Finally, the student and I agree upon what we will do next lesson. This is also very important. If they know what they will study next they are more incentivised to come back.

If you have some time left: Finisher activities

If you have any time left, finish your lesson with a bang using a high-energy finisher activity. See all our activities in chapter eight.

Feedback

Most platforms will require you to write feedback on your student after every lesson. If you are not organised this will become time consuming. To minimise writing time, I keep a library of grammar explanations on my computer. I then copy and paste them into the forms and personalise it with the student's name and a quick message for them. Organisation here is key or you will spend a good 15-20% of your time simply writing forms.

The structure of a lesson

In an hour's lesson, I usually cover at least one main grammar or vocabulary point followed by an easier language point that they have either studied before or can understand quickly.

A typical lesson looks like this:

10 minutes: Speaking about a podcast or answering a conversation question.

10 minutes: Content of last lesson reviewed (perhaps some drilling).

8 minutes: Introduction of grammar or vocabulary point.

8 minutes: Controlled speaking practice of above grammar or vocabulary point.

7 minutes: Freer speaking practice of above point.

5 minutes: Introduce second, easier grammar or vocabulary point.

6 minutes: Controlled speaking practice of the second language point.

3 minutes: Give homework. Talk about what you will study in the next lesson. Deal with questions.

3 minutes: High energy finishing activity (if there is time).

Other things to remember

Communicate with cognates

Cognates are words of a shared origin. The origin of most European languages (including English) is Latin. Therefore, when teaching speakers of these languages, the teacher should speak in Latin cognates for better communication.

For example, if you use a sentence such as, 'she couldn't put up with the situation,' few in the class would understand you. This is because 'put up with' is a phrasal verb made from Anglo Saxon words. What word could you use in place of 'put up with?' Right, 'tolerate'. 'Tolerate is a cognate derived from the Latin word 'tolerātus'. In Spanish it's 'tolerar' and in French 'tolérer' and so on. And so, if you say instead, 'she couldn't tolerate the situation' everyone will know what you're talking about.

This begs the question, 'how do you identify a Latin cognate?' Well, cognates are the longer, more formal words in English such as 'describe', 'originate', and 'create.' If you know another European language such as Spanish, Italian, French or Portuguese, they are the words that coincide between the two languages. If you're still unclear, there are lists available on the internet.

Don't talk too much

As the teacher, it is important to be mindful about how much you speak. You are there to feed your students information and correct their mistakes while they practice. Nothing more. Don't give your opinion about something they are discussing and don't talk about your personal life.

You already know how to speak English, now it's their turn to learn. 90% of the English spoken in your class should be produced by your students.

Individual classes vs group classes

You're likely find that one-on-one lessons online are not dissimilar to those that you would teach in the classroom. The teacher and student can chat just as they would in a physical space, they can use the messaging application as a whiteboard to clarify points and share pictures, role plays and other materials through the shared screen feature.

Teaching a group class online, however, is very different. The reason is that in a physical class, most speaking practice occurs through pair work. When your students practice together, they spend far more time speaking than if they had to wait their turn with the teacher.

This simply isn't possible in an online classroom because everyone would be talking over each other. Without pairs work, the teacher must initiate speaking. Student interaction is still possible (and I encourage you to facilitate it) but it happens within the group. For this reason, the teacher must keep tighter rein on the class to make sure that people do not talk over each other or, more likely, someone falls silent.

Here are some tips for successful online group classes.

Keep everyone involved

It sounds obvious but it is not as simple as you might think. Talking over the internet does not come naturally to everyone and it is easy to let others take control of the conversation, particularly when you can't see the faces of anyone you're speaking to.

For this reason, it is important that the teacher keeps all of their students contributing. They can do this by:

Quick fire questions: A pop quiz is a brilliant way to end a lesson with a bang or bring back laughter and energy to a class after completing something difficult. Choose a topic with which everyone is familiar and ask quick one-word- answer questions.

A good example would be the difference between 'make' and 'do'. The teacher says the noun such as 'the bed' and the student answers whether it's used with the verb 'make' or 'do' ('make the bed').

Having the teacher bark your name can be unsettling for some and so, to soften the experience, assign each student a number or a colour. Then, during the quiz, address the student by a number instead of their name when asking the question. For example:

Teacher: 'The washing. Two'

Sara (who is number two): 'Do'.

Note: Say the name (or number) of the student *after* the question, not before. That way you keep everyone thinking because no one knows who will be chosen to answer the question.

Chain activities: Chain stories are another effective way to get everyone participating. It is also good for inter-student interaction as the class must work as a team.

To start the chain story the teacher says a line. Student A must follow with a new line, based on what was said, using the same grammatical structure. Student B must follow on from Student A's line and so on, until the story no longer makes sense. Take a look at this example to practice the second conditional:

Teacher: If I owned a bike, I would cycle to work every day. Three.

John (who is three): If I cycled to work every day, I wouldn't need to go to the gym.

Teacher: One.

Lara (who is one): If I didn't need to go to the gym, how would I chat to that guy I fancy?

Note: Again, I recommend using the number system instead of names. You really keep students on their toes if you randomly pick numbers in formations such as one, four, three, two, two four and so on, often leading to someone bursting into laugher when they realise that their number has come up twice in a row.

Encourage interaction

Just because your students are not sitting in the same physical space does not mean that they cannot speak together. You'll find that the most interesting classes come from students discussing ideas with each other. This also takes the pressure off you and so you should encourage interaction wherever possible.

The icebreaker activity

The first step is to set up a proper getting-to-know-you session during your first lesson together. To help you, I have designed a two page work sheet(page 87) of ice breaker questions, separated by levels, which your students can ask each other. Place the sheet on your shared screen and allow your students to choose a few that interest them. Because this is still an English lesson, the question is not complete and the students must do the work to create a proper interrogative.

After the sheet, get your students to make up some further questions themselves based on what their classmates have said, exactly as if it were a face-to-face conversation.

After the icebreaker session, facilitate the group interaction in every activity. One way to do this is with group debates and roleplays. Because your students can't see each other, the teacher must manage the conversation with questions such as 'what do you think, Lara?' or 'John, what's your idea?' so that everyone gets a turn to speak.

Teaching group classes with different nationalities

You're far more likely to teach a class of different nationalities online then you are in a classroom. Some teachers may hesitate to allow too much interaction in case one student offends another. So far, this has not been my experience; English students are normally an educated, open-minded lot.

Getting people to talk about their part of the world is an enriching experience for the whole class, particularly when people start to compare in an open-minded, non-judgemental way how their respective countries tackle similar issues. If you prefer to steer clear of heavy subjects then comparing food culture, sport, history and even how people spend their free time can be just as interesting.

If you do find yourself with a student who makes stereotypical comments about other nationalities ask them about the stereotypes foreigners have of their own country. This is normally a polite way to shut them up.

Encourage interaction outside of class

In a physical class, students wouldn't talk only during a lesson, they would talk before it, after it and maybe even help each other with homework assignments or send each other lesson notes. This is the sort of relationship you should also encourage between your online students.

You can do this by setting up a Facebook page for your classes where students can ask questions on your 'wall'. You don't necessarily have to answer these questions yourself. Other students will hopefully answer them for you in the comments section below, which ends up becoming a discussion board.

Through your page, you can share extra materials, interesting articles or even schedule the next class.

The tips that turn a good teacher into a great teacher

1. Find out what your students want to study: What tenses are they having problems with? In what situations do they use their English? Do they have an English exam coming up?

2. Make lesson notes and share them with the class.

3. Listen out for mistakes and create lessons to fix them.

---

3. How to teach grammar and vocabulary: Oral drills

In my first book I talked about how oral drills were the most effective way to teach English. This is doubly so when teaching online. You couldn't teach from textbooks online even if you wanted to. You would have to ask your students to buy the same book and then sit there in a different space while they worked through the exercises. What would be the point of paying for a teacher?

I have seen some teachers try to recreate the textbook experience online by showing PowerPoint presentations on their shared screen. This may be slightly more interactive (if the teacher asks questions) but it is still slow and boring and provides limited opportunities for speaking practice.

I wonder why so many students put up with these types of classes. Perhaps it's because they've never experienced an oral drills lesson. They don't realise the fluidity they can achieve with classes provided by a teacher who challenges them and keeps them constantly speaking. These teachers are worth their weight in gold because, through them, students really can achieve the dream of speaking fluent English. They are teachers like you.

What is a drill?

When you were a child you learnt to speak your native language by listening and repeating sentences spoken by the adults around you. Over time you built up these sentences to be able to speak in the past, the present, the future, hypothetically and so on. From about the age of 10 you were a master of the language and could say everything you wanted to say without even thinking about it.

This is what drills lessons are designed to do. The teacher takes a piece of grammar and, through questions or statements, gets the student to reproduce different sentences until the words come out of their mouths with minimal thought. Then they move on to the next grammar point.

Take a look at this example to practice the present perfect and past simple.

Teacher: Ask me how many coffees I have drunk today.

Student: How many coffees have you drunk today?

Teacher: I have drunk two coffees today. And you?

Student: I have drunk three coffees today.

Teacher: And yesterday?

Student: I drank four coffees yesterday.

Teacher: How many emails have you written to Madonna?

Student: I have never written an email to Madonna.

Teacher: And your sister?

Student: She has never written an email to Madonna either.

How many language points did the student practice here? Well, the interrogative (questions), negative with 'never' third person with the reference to a sister, the past, the present perfect and 'either.'

Not bad considering this practice would have lasted less than two minutes. Imagine what you can do in an hour and a half.

Drills are the closest thing we have to reproducing the way we all learnt our native languages, but of course, in a condensed period of time.

Teaching individuals: Ask the teacher

In this section we will learn how to use drills in one-on-one lessons. If a teacher continually gets a student to answer questions then the student never gets to practice questions themselves.

Remember that questions are difficult in English because the subject and the verb swap places, ('she has eaten an apple today' becomes 'has she eaten an apple today?') or you have to insert the auxiliary verbs 'do' or 'does'. Trust me, they're hard.

It is therefore better to get the student to ask you questions. This technique is called 'ask the teacher.'

'Ask the teacher' works like this: you feed your student a variety of questions to ask you. You answer and then you shoot the question straight back at them with an 'and you?' or to practice the third person 'and your sibling/boss/friend/partner/neighbour?'

They then answer with the appropriate construction and you move onto the next question.

By asking the student to ask you, the sentence is in a straight statement form. It is therefore the student who must reorder the words or add a 'do/does' to make the question. For example:

Teacher: Ask me whose computer I am using.

This is a statement. The student must then swap the subject pronoun and to be verb around to make:

Student: Whose computer are you using?

Before you begin it is important to find out whether your student has siblings, a boss, neighbours, and so on. Not everyone has a romantic partner or friends and so I would steer clear of these topics until you know them better. Also, people often have strong feelings about their parents (both positive and negative) and so I would avoid them as a reference in your classes.

The best people to use to practice the third person are brothers and sisters. If your student has no siblings ask them to name someone in their life that you can use as a substitute; a cousin perhaps or an aunt or uncle.

Finally, you should also explain that 'ask the teacher' is to help the student practice questions, and not because you are an ego maniac who only wants to talk about yourself.

Ask the teacher to practice vocabulary

You have lots of questions at your disposal when practicing vocabulary. With each question, work one of the words you are practicing into the sentence along with a variety of tenses and question structures.

Ask questions appropriate to your student's level. There is no point asking questions in second conditional if they haven't studied it yet. If your student is at a high level, make sure that the tenses you choose challenge them.

Take a look at this example to practice medical vocabulary with the words: twist, painkiller, plaster cast and break. The student is at an intermediate level

Teacher: Ask me if I have ever broken my wrist.

Student: Have you ever broken your wrist?

Teacher: Yes, I have broken my wrist. And you?

Student: No, I have never broken my wrist.

Teacher: Ask me how long I had to wear a plaster cast for.

Student: How long did you have to wear a plaster cast for?

Teacher: I had to wear a plaster cast for 6 weeks. Ask me, if I used to twist my ankle a lot when I was young.

Student: Did you use to twist your ankle a lot when you were young?

Teacher: No, I didn't use to twist my ankle a lot when I was young. And your sister?

Student: She didn't use to twist her ankle a lot when she was young but she did twist her ankle once.

Teacher: Ask me when the last time I took a painkiller was.

Student: When was the last time you took a painkiller?

How many structures did the teacher include here? It's five: Have you ever, never, how long + past, used to, when was the last time.

Ask the teacher: to practice grammar

As you're practicing one language point only, you won't be able to use the same range of grammar. However, you can vary the questions and/ or tenses for a challenging practice.

Take a look at this example to practice 'to get used to + verb in gerund'. Here the language point allows us to practice a range of tenses.

Teacher: Ask me if <u>I am getting</u> used to internet shopping.

Student: Are you getting used to internet shopping?

Teacher: Yes, I am slowly getting used to internet shopping. And you?

Student: No, I haven't got used to internet shopping yet.

More examples:

Teacher: Ask me if my boss <u>has got used</u> to driving in the city. (Follow up question) And your boss?

Teacher: Ask me if I <u>will get used</u> to being retired. (Follow up question) And your parents?

Teacher: Ask me if I <u>would get used</u> to living without the internet if there were an apocalypse. (Follow up question) And your neighbours?

How many tenses did the teacher cover here? It's four. The present continuous, the present perfect, future with 'will' and the second conditional.

Other language points limit you to one tense, but you can still practice a range of questions. Take a look at this example with the present perfect.

Language point: The present perfect

Teacher: Ask me <u>how many</u> apples I have eaten today.

Student: How many apples have you eaten today?

Teacher: I haven't eaten any apples today. And you?

Student: I have eaten one apple today.

More examples...

Teacher: Ask me <u>how much</u> exercise I have done today. (Follow up question) And your flatmate?

Teacher: Ask me if <u>I have ever</u> visited New York. (And your mother?)

Teacher: Ask me <u>how often</u> I have seen Donald Trump in the news today. (And your boss?)

Teacher: Ask me <u>how long</u> I have been a football fan? (And your best friend?)

How many different types of questions did the student practice? It's five: how many, how much, how often, have you ever and how long.

Question starters for ask the teacher

Here is a list of question starters for 'ask the teacher'. Remember to add the third person by saying not just 'ask me how often I...' but also 'ask me how often my brother/sister....'

Always throw the question back to the student so they can answer for themselves. Practice the third person, 'they' and 'we' by asking 'and your sister' and 'your work colleagues' 'and your neighbours' and so on.

Level Beginner

If I am...

If my brother/ sister is

If my neighbours are

How often I (or my brother/sister etc)

How much [insert word] I...(or my brother/sister etc)

How many [insert word] I...

Where I was born...

If I was...

If my parents were...

If I usually...

How often my brother usually...

If my neighbour can...

Level Intermediate

If I have ever...

How far [insert destination] is from my house...

If my sister ever...

If I am [insert verb in gerund] right now... (e.g. If I am eating an orange right now).

If my sister was [insert verb in gerund] yesterday...

If I would ever....

How often my brother used to...

When the last time my sister [insert word] was?

Whose [insert word] I am using now...

If you should...

If the government must...

If I will [insert verb] if...

If my brother is going to...

How long I have been [insert verb in gerund]....

How long my sister has [insert participle of verb]...

Level Upper intermediate - advanced

If I have already...

If my cat used to...

If my cat is getting used to...

How long it takes me to....

How long it used to take my sister to...

How long a [insert word] lasts

How long my last [insert word] lasted

What [insert word] is like...

What [insert name of person or thing] looks like...

What [insert name of person or thing] sounds/ tastes like...

If I would [insert verb] if....

If I would have [insert verb if...]

Teaching groups: Ask each other

If you practiced 'ask the teacher' in a group, your students would spend most of their time waiting for their turn. As a teacher produces dynamic, high-energy classes, this is not what you want. Instead, involve as many students as you can by feeding them questions to ask each other.

Take a look at this example with four students: Sarah, Lara, John and Stewart. They are practicing technology vocabulary: To download, laptop, keyboard, social networks. They are an upper-intermediate level.

Teacher: Stuart, ask Sarah if she would use a social network if she didn't own a mobile phone.

Stuart: Sarah, would you use a social network if you didn't own a mobile phone?

Sarah: Yes, I would still use a social network if I didn't own a mobile phone.

Teacher: Sarah, ask Lara what her keyboard <u>looks like.</u>

Sarah: What does your keyboard look like?

Lara: My keyboard is black and plastic.

Teacher: And your sister's keyboard?

Lara: Her keyboard is white.

Teacher: Lara, ask John if he <u>would get used to</u> downloading films if he didn't own a laptop.

And so on. Notice that because these students are a high level the teacher has embedded the vocabulary into difficult language points to make the exercise more challenging. What tenses has the teacher used? The second conditional, to look like and to get used to + the second conditional.

In group sessions the teacher should still throw the question back to the student every now and again with a 'and your boss?' or 'and your favourite actor?' to mix it up and keep the class on their toes.

Types of drills

So now that you've had a taste of how oral drills work, let me show you a few different types of drills you have at your disposal.

Drills fall into two categories: closed drills where there is only one right answer and open drills where the student is free to make up the rest of the sentence as long as it is in the correct tense. Below I shall give you examples of both.

Closed drills

The passive voice

We make the passive voice with an object, some version of 'to be' verb and the participle.

For example, 'The apple was eaten,' or 'The painting is finished.'

We use passive voice when we want to emphasise the result of an action rather than the person or subject doing the action.

For example, in the active sentence 'I did the report,' it is me who is important in the sentence and the fact that *I did* it. Change this to passive and it becomes, 'The report was done, by me.' The report is now the important part of the sentence.

The passive voice drill

You say an active voice sentence below and the student must change it to passive voice. If there is a preposition between the verb and object you keep the preposition after the verb.

Teacher: The girl ruined her dress.

Student: The dress <u>was ruined</u> by the girl.

Teacher: She is painting the wall.

Student: The wall <u>is being painted</u>.

Teacher: They have thought of a solution.

Student: A solution <u>has been thought</u> of.

How many passive voice tenses has the teacher covered here? It's three. Passive voice in past ('was ruined', in present continuous ('is painting') and present perfect ('has been thought of').

You can in fact use the passive voice with all tenses and a good drill should cover all the tenses your class knows to illustrate all the possible variations.

Here are some more drills. What is the passive version of these sentences?

- o She will take the chair.
- o They were thinking about the problem.
- o I have chosen a new member of staff.
- o They shook the tree.

o   He used to make a call every day.
o   She should order the coffee machine by the end of the week.

Short Answers

Short Answers are when someone answers with the same auxiliary used in the question. For example, 'Is your sister going to Italy next year? Short answer: 'Yes she is.' This is easy to explain and a good high-energy drill to finish your class.

Short answer drill

Practice by giving your students a question and getting them to answer with a 'yes' or 'no' + auxiliary verb. Watch out for questions with 'Do you have' and make sure they answer 'Yes I do/no I don't' instead of 'Yes I have / no I haven't' For example, 'do you have a car?' 'Yes, I do.'

Teacher: Are you Italian?

Student: No, I'm not

Teacher: Is your father Italian?

Student: Yes, he is.

Teacher: Do you have a microwave?

Student: No, I don't.

Teacher: Did you do something interesting yesterday?

Student: Yes, I did.

More examples:

o   Should you smoke?
o   Have you caught a bus today?
o   Did you use to wear a uniform at school?
o   Will it snow next January?
o   Is it snowing now?
o   Would your sister accept 50 euros if I gave it to her?

Open drills

Open drills, as the name suggests, give your students a statement and allow them to invent the answer as long as it is in the correct tense. Take a look at some examples below.

The second conditional

The second conditional, also known as the present conditional, refers to something hypothetical but possible.

Its structure runs:

If + past + would + infinitive (no to)

Practice by giving your students a statement that is not true. They have to turn it into a second conditional 'if' clause, and invent the second part.

For example, the teacher knows that John can't speak German.

Teacher: 'You speak German.'

John: 'If I spoke German, I would look for a job in Germany.'

Teacher: 'And with contraction?'

John: 'If I spoke German, I'd look for a job in Germany.'

Sentences
- You play [insert instrument].
- You speak [insert language].
- You buy a Ferrari.
- You are a politician.
- You see a famous footballer in your local supermarket.
- Your brother/sister writes a best-selling novel.

- Your friends make you go bungee jumping.
- You know how to fly a helicopter.
- There is a party in the room next door.
- You see a robbery.
- There is an earthquake in your town.
- You forget your mother's birthday.

Third conditional

This time practice by giving your students a statement about the past that is not true. They have to turn it into a third conditional 'if' clause and invent the second part.

For example, the teacher knows that Sarah didn't grow up in the USA.

Teacher: 'You grew up in the USA.'

Sarah: 'If I had grown up in the USA, I would have gone to school there.'

Teacher: 'And with contraction?'

John: 'If I'd grown up in the USA, I'd have gone to school there.'

Sentences

- o   You grew up in the USA.
- o   You went to Tokyo last week.
- o   You forgot your keys this morning.
- o   There was a marathon in your city yesterday.
- o   You accidentally threw out your wallet in the trash yesterday.
- o   Your parents had 10 children.

Provided that and as long as

'Provided that' and 'as long as' connect two clauses of a conditional sentence together (either the zero, first, second or third conditional). They mean 'if this happens, I will do that.' For example: 'I would buy a new car provided that I got the job' or 'She would study chemistry as long as you bought the books.'

Provided that and as long as drill

Practice by giving your student the first part of the sentence and elicit the second half. Your student can answer with anything they like as long as it makes sense and is in the correct tense.

For example, the teacher may say 'I would drive...' and the student answers with 'I would drive as long as you <u>paid</u> for the petrol.' Make sure your student uses the correct conditional form. 'I would drive as long as you <u>pay</u> for the petrol,' mixes the first and second conditional and is not correct.

Teacher: She would look after your dog...

Student: She <u>would</u> look after your dog as long as it <u>behaved</u> itself.

Teacher: They will make the cake...

Student: They <u>will</u> make the cake provided that you <u>buy</u> the ingredients.

Teacher: There won't be too many issues...

Student: There <u>won't</u> be too many issues as long as we <u>arrive</u> on time.

Teacher: She would learn to play the piano...

Student: She <u>would</u> learn to play the piano provided that you <u>learnt</u> to play the drums.

More examples:

- o   I will cut down on caffeine...
- o   He would take up tennis...
- o   They could tolerate the noise...
- o   We won't complain...
- o   She would see the film again...
- o   They will build more houses...

Unless

'Unless' also connects two conditional clauses. Broadly speaking, it is the opposite of 'as long as' and 'provided that.' It means 'I won't do that until this happens.'

Now do the same thing with 'unless'. For example, the teacher says 'They won't study Chinese...' and elicits something like 'They won't study Chinese unless they move to China.'

Unless practice

To practice, give your students the first clause of the sentence and ask them to make up the second with 'unless.' Make sure that your students end it with the correct conditional form. 'They won't study Chinese unless they went to China', mixes two conditionals and is not correct.

Teacher: They won't study Chinese...

Student: They <u>won't</u> study Chinese unless they <u>go</u> to China.

Teacher: He wouldn't join the army...

Student: He <u>wouldn't</u> join the army unless <u>there were</u> a war.

Teacher: She won't live in a flat...

Student: She <u>won't</u> live in a flat unless <u>it's</u> in the right neighbourhood.

More examples:

- o We won't arrive on time...
- o They wouldn't bring up the subject...
- o We wouldn't eat insects...
- o He won't have children...
- o They wouldn't take out a mortgage...
- o She won't attend the wedding...

Model verbs in past: Deduction and possibility

Model verbs in past are one of the toughest language points to teach.

In the present tense, 'must' makes a positive deduction, for example, 'He <u>must be</u> a policeman, he is wearing the uniform,' and 'can't' the negative. 'He <u>can't be</u> a policeman, he is robbing a bank.'

This idea continues in past by adding 'have' + participle.

For example, 'He <u>must have been</u> a policeman, he wore the uniform' and, 'He <u>can't have been</u> a policeman, he robbed a bank.'

Because 'can' is such a strange and irregular verb you can also say, 'He <u>couldn't have been</u> a policeman.'

Possibility is expressed with 'may' and 'might,' for example, 'She <u>may be</u> a famous athlete (she looks fit and I just saw her signing autographs)' and in negative 'She <u>might not be</u> a famous athlete (I just saw her scoffing a McDonald's).'

Again, this continues in past with 'may'/ 'might' + 'have' + participle.'

For example, 'She <u>might have been</u> a famous athlete, I saw her signing autographs,' or, 'She <u>may not have been</u> a famous athlete, she used to eat a lot of McDonald's.'

Model verbs in past: deduction and possibility drill

Give your students one of the following sentences and ask them to make a positive and negative deduction and a possibility statement with 'may or might.' Your students can answer with anything they like as long as it makes sense and it's in the right tense.

Teacher: He cycled to work and he didn't have a driver's licence.

Stewart: He <u>couldn't have driven</u> a car.

Teacher: And in positive?

Lara: He <u>must have been</u> fit.

Teacher: And a possibility?

John: He <u>might have failed</u> his driving test.

Sarah: He <u>might not have liked</u> cars.

Teacher: She wore a crown and was married to the king.

Sarah: She <u>must have been</u> the queen.

Teacher: And in negative?

John: She <u>couldn't have been</u> poor.

Teacher: And a possibility?

Lara: She <u>might have been</u> powerful.

Stewart: She <u>might not have wanted</u> to be queen.

More examples

- o He cycled to work and he didn't have a driver's licence (deduction: he didn't drive a car).
- o She was allergic to dogs and didn't like them (deduction: she didn't have a dog).
- o He bought a new car every year.
- o They spoke Dutch and lived in the Netherlands.
- o The boat did not arrive at the port. It has disappeared (deduction: it sank or got lost).
- o He spent a lot of time in hospital.

And finally

So now you understand how drills work and what they can do for your English class, you may be wondering where you find more. Well there is a book that provides drills and/or speaking exercises for every grammar point. That book is called The Ultimate ESL Teaching Manual, written by your author.

Each drills exercise contains at least 12 example sentences. Study and use them, then when you're ready write more to add variation to your classes.

Drills are without doubt the best way to learn grammar and vocabulary, but they are only half the story. For a truly great lesson, your students need a way to explore the language point for themselves through freer speaking practice. Welcome to the next chapter.

4. Speaking practice

Drills provide the training to memorise and refine new language points, but if you want your students to learn to speak fluently (and of course you do) then you really have to let them off the leash to explore the idea for themselves.

In the ESL world there are five main speaking activities. These are roleplays, debates, story-telling, describing pictures, and games. I will explore each in more detail below.

Speaking activities online

Your students pay you to listen to them speak and so you should dedicate the same amount of time to speaking practice online as you would in a physical class. However, because most online lessons are with individuals, they don't last as long as they would with a group class in a physical space. For example, a 20 minute speaking activity in a classroom would last no more than 10 minutes in an online session. You must therefore factor this in when planning your lessons.

Another thing to consider is that because you cannot use body language or a blackboard, getting an idea across is more difficult online than in a physical space. All explanations for speaking activities must therefore be kept short and very simple.

Roleplays

Roleplays are short situations which allow a student a certain language function, (such as setting up a bank account), or grammar or vocabulary point. They are my preferred speaking activity. My first reason for this is that they are creative. Using one's imagination is fun and interesting. Roleplays transport students out of their normal lives and explore a different, more playful side of themselves. Executed correctly, most students will have a good time.

But, great roleplays don't come from thin air. You've got to set them up correctly to get the maximum engagement from your class or they will fall flat.

Setting up an online roleplay

The concept of a roleplay should be no more than three lines and very simple in both online and offline classes. However, in an online class this is especially true.

Your students view lines and lines of information about their 'roles' as a waste of time and they will be reluctant to take part in anything they don't completely understand.

However, they will appreciate a simple, purposeful roleplay as a way to practice their language skills.

In a classroom, the teacher sets the scene through questions to get students thinking about the situation before they start the roleplay.

This can also be achieved online. For example, for a roleplay about choosing a holiday, the teacher could post a list of questions in the messages section such as:

o   What's the best way to find information about holidays?
o   What's the worst holiday you've ever been on?

The next and vital step for a successful roleplay is to engage your students to make the task work by coming up with ideas for the situation themselves. A teacher can also achieve this online through simple questions.

For example, take a look at the 'choosing a holiday' roleplay. To make a student part of the roleplay, ask them to name:

o   A destination they would most like to visit
o   A destination they would least like to visit

Then take this information and add it to your roleplay. To show you what I mean, take a look at the final 'choosing a holiday' roleplay below.

> There is a travel agent and a client. The client wants to book a holiday to [insert name of students' dream destination here] but the travel agent wants to sell them a holiday to [insert name of students' nightmare destination here].

Another top tip is not to take it too seriously. Encourage humour by feeding your student an amusing situation. A bit of laughter should ease any performance anxiety.

Roleplays for single students

I have written all the short roleplays I use, together with some questions to get your student involved. I confess I don't have roleplays for every grammar point but there are thirteen to choose from.

You'll find them in the worksheets section on page 107, ready for you to copy and paste into the messages section. These roleplays are written for one student only, to practice with the teacher. However, with a bit of imagination, you could adapt them for small groups of two to three students.

Roleplays for group classes

The Ultimate ESL Online Teaching Manual also offers six roleplays for group classes. You'll also find these in the worksheets section, ready to display on your class shared screen.

Each roleplay contains:

- o Four to five warm-up questions to set the scene. Feel free to adapt these to suit the experiences of your class, or invent some more.
- o Roles for four students. These are sparsely described. Ask your students each to invent their character's motivations and briefly describe their position before the roleplay begins.
- o A two-person alternative for an individual class. The teacher takes one role and the student the other.

In this chapter, you'll find a brief description of each roleplay and a list of suggested language points to use with the activity, along with example sentences.

Six Roleplays

Roleplay one: The theme park mascot

A young worker is spending the summer working as a theme park mascot, but they are not happy and want to change to the park's fast food restaurant. Their manager, however, does not want to move them.

Suggested Language points to practice: 'Get + adjective' or 'to get used to'. For example:

Manager: You'll get used to running around in the heat.

Young worker: No, I'm getting sweaty and yesterday I got dizzy.

Roleplay two: The Erasmus Student from Hell

After many years together these Erasmus students don't want to live together anymore. They both think that the other is anti-social and has bad habits. One flatmate did something very annoying the previous year; explain it to them using 'wish.'

Suggested language practice: Wish and hope, 'to be used to' and 'to get used to'. For example:

Student A: I wish you would clean the shower sometimes, can't get used to the smell.

Student B: I wish you hadn't invited your crazy cousin to stay last year. He destroyed the kitchen.

Roleplay three: The press conference

It's sometime in the future and your city is facing serious environmental problems. The people call a press conference with the mayor to discuss how these problems are impacting on their lives and how the government plans to solve the problem.

Suggested language practice: Future perfect, conditionals. For example:

Journalist: Scientists predict that by 2050 the city will have flooded. What can we do about this?

Mayor: Well, we plan to build a sea wall. It should have been built by 2049.

Roleplay four: Making a movie

A director is looking for locations to make a movie. Two ambassadors try to persuade the director to make the film in their respective countries, but the director has doubts about what they're offering.

Suggested language points to practice: Quantifiers (so, so many, so much, too many, too much, too + adjective) and enough. For example:

Ambassador: My country has mountains and a desert which is perfect for your western.

Director: But I'm not sure it's <u>safe enough</u>. There are <u>so many</u> bandits.

Roleplay five: City planners

Air quality in the city is worse than ever. For this reason, city planners are proposing making the inner city a car free zone. The mayor, an owner of a large business, a resident and a journalist discuss the pros and cons of the idea.

Suggested language points: Second conditional, unless and as long as. For example:

Mayor: We could close the inner city to cars <u>as long as there was</u> a car park where people could leave their vehicles when they entered.

Owner of department store: You couldn't build a car park <u>unless you knocked down</u> some buildings.

Roleplay six: Starbucks on Mars.

Humans set up a colony on Mars 80 years ago and the population has grown to 6000 people. Starbucks would like to set up a coffee shop. If approved, Starbucks would be the first chain business to enter the colony. Members of the colony discuss the pros and cons of the Starbuck representative's offer.

Suggested language point to practice: Even if + conditional and even though + indicative. For example:

Local resident: Even though we have lots of entertainment facilities, people are getting bored.

Small business owner: Even if you allowed Starbucks on the planet, how do we know they'll improve the local economy?

Debates

Debates are a useful speaking exercise for ESL students as it's important to have the phrases and grammar to be able to express your opinion. Moreover, many English language exams such as the IELTS require a student to provide their opinion on a range of topics.

For a successful debate your students must be at least a B1 level or above. Lower levels simply wouldn't have the breadth of language to be able to express themselves properly.

Debate preparation

Before you begin, identify the vocabulary that you want to use. The main language you'll want to practice is opinion phrases and connectors for structuring an argument (see a basic table below). Don't hand your student the words on a plate; elicit from them what they need.

Check that they understand the meanings by asking them to give you example sentences. If your student is a higher level, they will want to practice more interesting phrases, a list of which you can find in the Connector worksheets on page 101

A basic phrase table

Opinion	Agree/disagree	Structuring	Conclusion
In my opinion	I agree/don't agree	In addition	To sum up
If I were them	That's rubbish	However	To recap
As far as I know	Let's compromise	Although	In conclusion
I believe/think		Firstly, secondly	
I am in favour of		Finally	

On top of this there may be a vocabulary topic you want to practice such as politics, environment or economics. This should be vocabulary that you have already studied in previous lessons. A debate is not the time to learn new words, but rather to practice the vocabulary you already know.

Setting up a debate

In a classroom environment, the teacher would probably divide students into teams to defend each side of an argument. Online, however, you'll probably be teaching one student and so the student must have this debate with themselves.

Step one: Prepare your student for the topic before the lesson

Select an interesting TED talk and ask your student to watch it for homework. Ask them to write down a few points for either side of the argument.

How to choose your debate topic

1# Centre your debate around a vocabulary topic you have just covered in class.

2# Use your common sense and steer clear of contentious subjects such as race relations, religion or anything that is going to embarrass one of your students.

3# Video content is better than articles because it is more dynamic and provides students with the opportunity to practice comprehension skills.

4# Great sources for video content include TedTalks found on www.ted.com, and the Vice or Economist channel on YouTube, which publishes current affairs content.

5# Any video should be no longer than 10 minutes because your students will have to watch it several times to understand the content. You, as the moderator, will of course have to watch it also.

Step two: Debate preparation in class

Next, check that the student has seen the video and ask them to explain the main arguments. Ask if anyone has a personal experience with this subject or has read anything about it in the news. Ask them to recount stories; do the groundwork to get them fired up and speaking about it in the debate.

Now elicit opinions and connectors, phrases and any other vocabulary you plan to use and write them on a Word document on the shared screen.

Step three: Use agree/ disagree statements instead of questions

Finally give your student two or three phrases about the topic with the statement 'agree or disagree' next to it. For example, 'Marijuana legalisation provides more benefits than problems for society. Agree or disagree.'

You'll find that agree or disagree statements are far more effective at getting people to speak than a 'do you think…' statement.

Step four: The debate

Ask your students to explain to you their ideas, structuring their argument with the connector words. Encourage them to explore the counter argument using phrases such as 'on the other hand' or 'however.' If they have a speaking exam coming up, presenting a counter argument as well will award them more marks than if they simply gave their opinion. If your student runs out of ideas, prompt them with a 'devil's advocate' question.

Quick debates

A debate doesn't have to be a huge activity, requiring mountains of preparation. You can actually create one from almost nothing as a fun five minute speaking activity at the end of the lesson. The same rules apply however; you must have a language objective in mind before you start. Focus your student by eliciting the words from them.

You're not limited to the same connectors. Take a look at the Connectors worksheets on page 101 . From these you can elicit vocabulary for referencing a source, expressing certainty, expressing doubt, expressing your honest opinion and so on.

Ask your student to pick a couple of choice phrases from a few of the categories and give them points every time they work one into the argument.

The crazy debate

Not all debates have to be heavy. Some of the most successful interactions are found with trivial subjects. The crazy debate is a light, no preparation activity, guaranteed to get some laughs.

Give your student two ideas, for example cycling vs the bus and, using your connectors. Ask them to defend cycling while you advocate the bus in a three minute debate. For example:

John: 'Cycling is better because it's cheaper.'

Teacher: 'Yes, however, the bus requires less energy. In addition, you don't arrive at your destination all sweaty.'

The student competes against his/herself to see how many of their selected phrases they can use in 90 seconds. Do this for at least three rounds.

Other mad debate topics include: 'peanut butter vs jam, 'cats or dogs', 'burgers or salad', 'smart phone or tablet.'

The crazy debate in a group class: Use your Connectors sheet on page 101 and 102 and ask your student to randomly select phrases using their corresponding number.

Two students start the debate. If they don't use any of their phrases within 20 seconds, or they make an error, the next student takes their place and so on. The debate ends once all the phrases are used or all ideas are exhausted. Then continue onto the next topic.

General debate questions

These are a set of general questions for debates. There is no right or wrong answer. Questions can be found in the worksheets section page xxx

Question sheets

Questions are also an effective way to practice a grammar point. I recommend using agree or disagree statements as it provokes more conversation. For example: for the vocabulary topic of the environment, an example question could be:

Water shortages are the biggest environmental problem facing cities. Agree/disagree.

Describe a photo

Images add colour and life to a class. In physical classrooms, teachers explain ideas through drawings on the whiteboard, diagrams or pictures in worksheets. In an online classroom, you can use images also by displaying them on your shared screen.

The worksheet section has over fifty images at your disposal that you can use for activities. Here are some ideas.

Compare and contrast: Take two photos and ask your student to use comparative adjectives, quantifiers (so, such, so many, so much, too, too many, too much) and modifiers (very, really, quite, incredibly, absolutely, rather) to make comparisons between the pictures.

For example, 'Lying on a beach is more relaxing than hiking but there are not as many opportunities to exercise'. Images for this task: Comparisons worksheets, World map.

Make 10 questions about the image: Give your student three minutes to come up with as many questions as they can about a photo. Give them extra points for creativity and breadth.

Images for this task: What does the future hold? I and II, What did the past used to be Like? Are you getting used to it, could you get used to it? Present continuous, Deduction and speculation worksheets.

Appearance, personality and emotions vocabulary: Ask your student to describe the appearance and the feelings of the people. Why do you imagine they feel this way?

Images for this task: Character cards, Appearance and personality and Reflexives worksheet.

Name as many objects as you can that begin with the letter...: Ask your student to name as many objects as they can, beginning with a chosen letter or which are a specified colour.

Images for this task: Food and drink, Prepositions of place Pronouns and Yet and already worksheets.

Think of as many adjectives as possible: Ask your students to think of as many adjectives as possible to describe a scene. Next go through the list and ask them to name the opposite adjective. This is a good one for lower levels.

Images for this task: Comparisons, just/just about to and Had better worksheets.

Just/Just about to..: Ask students what they think had just happened before the picture was taken and what they think is just about to happen.

Images for this task: Just/Just about to, Movements and Deduction and speculation worksheets.

It would be a disaster if../it would be more exciting if...: Practice the second conditional by asking your students what would turn the scene into a disaster or make it more exciting. Give extra points for imaginative answers. For example, 'it would be a disaster if aliens landed in the middle of the market square now.'

Images for this task: comparison, what does the future hold II, Deduction and speculation and Present continuous worksheets.

Creating stories

Creating stories is an effective way to practice past tenses, obscure vocabulary or irregular verbs. In an online class, you must tell the story in a chain. In a one-on-one class the teacher and student, bat the story back and forth between them. In a group class, this would happen between the students.

To start the chain, one student provides the first line (once upon a time there was...), and the next student continues, and so on. The teacher manages who goes next by saying the student's name or number. In an individual class the teacher and student take turns to forward the story.

What to practice

Before you start, decide what you want to practice. One of the most effective language points for this exercise is irregular verbs.

Display one of the irregular verb sheets on your shared screen and tell your class that their story must include all of these verbs in a past tense. Each verb can only be used once. For this reason, you'll wish to 'cross off' each verb as it is used. As this isn't possible on a PDF document you can also download these sheets in Word format from the book's site bilinguanation.com.

Stories are also a good way of practicing vocabulary which is difficult to fit into roleplays and debates; things like movement verbs (jump, snore, sneeze, lift, slash and so on).

How to start a story

Method one: Yes and no exercise

Explain to your student(s) that they are going to invent a story. Tell them to ask you five questions about the setting and plot to which you can only answer 'yes' or 'no'. For example:

Sarah: 'Is it set underwater?'

Teacher: 'Yes.'

Sarah: 'Are there pirates?'

Teacher: 'No.'

Using this information your students must now make a story. Give them a few minutes to think of some ideas and start the chain.

Method two: Occupation, location, object and year

Ask your student(s) to think of an occupation, location, object and year and construct the story from these ideas. For example, 'once upon a time there was a plumber who lived in New York city...' (the opening to a Super Mario Brothers story).

Method three: Rory's Story Cubes

Rory's Story Cubes are 9 dice which carry symbols instead of numbers. The idea is that you roll the dice and make a story from whatever appears. The Story Cubes also have a desktop app version (as well as tablet and other devices) which means you can 'roll' the dice on your shared screen and use the symbols to create an idea for a story. For more structure, combine the occupation, location, object and year method also.

Method four: Use pictures from the worksheets

Show your student a picture from one of the worksheets and ask them to use it as the basis of a story.

5. Games and other speaking activities

Games are a good way to end a lesson on a fun note. It is important that your students leave the lesson feeling positive and upbeat, particularly if it has been a difficult one, so that they'll look forward to the next class.

Here is a list of fun activities and games for online study.

One: Tongue twisters

Tongue twisters are a great way to practice enunciation. There are many famous ones out there on the internet and also in this book. Give each student a tongue twister and one minute to practice. Next each student says their line. The winner is the one with the fewest errors. You'll find Tongue twisters' worksheet on page 130.

Two: Fortunately/ Unfortunately

This is from another improv game. The teacher and student forms a chain speech. In a group class, the students do this between them. Each of participant must begin with the line 'Fortunately...' And then the next continues with 'Unfortunately...' and so on until you run out of ideas. This mix of positive and negative comments can lead to some very funny improvisations.

To start, give your students a situation, for example: 'The inauguration of a new school,' 'a boss telling their employees about a new development in the company,' 'parents telling their kids they're going to move house,' and so on.

Next, agree on some vocabulary, phrases or grammar tenses they have to work into the speech. Finally, get your strongest student to start the chain and see what happens. If you wish, you could give them a time limit.

Suggested language point to practice: Even if/even though. For example, 'fortunately, even though you have to leave your school, there is a lovely one near the new house. Unfortunately, even if there were places you couldn't go there because it's a private school and we don't have the money to pay for it.'

Three: What's the problem?

This is a good game for practicing modal verbs in present and past. The teacher (or another student in a group class) has a problem, but doesn't know what it is. They must work out what the problem is from the questions people are asking them.

In a group class you must first, select the student who has the problem. Then send the rest of the class the problem through a private communication channel, such as email. To spice it up, you can also assign roles; one student gives good advice, another bad advice, another crazy advice. If your students are only at a basic level, however, you may want to stick with everyone giving good advice.

Next, give the student (or class in a group class) five minutes to deliver their advice. Finally, the teacher or 'problem' student (in a group class) must guess what the problem is. For example, if they were agoraphobic, some advice may be 'you should get a dog and walk it in the park every day,' or 'you don't have to go far, just a few steps around the block.'

You can also adapt this game to practice modal verbs in past with an old problem. For example, if the problem was someone lost their girlfriend because they spent too much time at the gym, the advice may be: 'You should have listened to your girlfriend more,' or 'You shouldn't have competed in that weight lifting contest.'

Four: The press conference

This game is only possible in a group class. It is similar to 'What's the problem?' One of your students is taking a press conference, but they don't know what it's about. The rest of your students are journalists. Through the journalists' questions, the interviewee must guess why they called the press conference. This is a good way to practice questions and almost any tense of your choice.

For example, if you wanted to practice present perfect continuous, questions may be, 'How long have you been interested in dinosaurs for?' or 'How often have you been taking them for walks?'

Five: Prefixes and suffixes:

Use the worksheet on page 115 to practice prefixes and suffixes. Give your student a root word such as 'taste' or 'occupy' and ask them to use as many prefixes and/or suffixes as possible to make a new word. Give them two minutes to do this.

Afterwards, conduct a pop quiz on what the most interesting words mean and ask them to make example sentences. Some root words to start you off: Taste, occupy, direct, employ, use, friend, normal, state, courage, hope.

6. How to teach questions

Compared to other European languages, questions in English are hard. The subject and the verb swap places, there is the added 'do' or 'does' and prepositions go at the end. For example, it is not 'about what are you thinking?' It is, 'what are you thinking about?'

Trust me, for speakers of other languages this is all very strange. For this reason, you must make question practice an integral part of every lesson. You don't have to spend a long time on it, but ten minutes practice towards the end of the lesson will make a huge difference to your students' English.

Here is how to do it.

Instead of asking a question, the teacher says the answer and asks their students to work out what the question was. To get the right question the teacher must emphasise the most important part of the sentence with their voice. For example:

Teacher: She goes running with *her sister*. What is the question?'

Student: 'Who does she go running with?'

Without this emphasis, the student could have easily asked, 'What is she doing?' which would be grammatically correct but not the question the teacher was searching for.

Below, I have written common statements for all main grammar points. There is a particular emphasis on the questions that students find the most difficult, such as prepositions at the end of sentences.

You can find a similar list in the original book, The Ultimate ESL Teaching Manual, but to give you more scope all statements here are completely new. Once you familiarise yourself with the technique I encourage you to write more.

Basic questions for A1 plus level

It is purple – *'What colour is it?'*

There are *five photos on the shelf* – *'How many photos are there on the shelf?'*

I *don't* know how to cook Chinese food – *'Do you know how to cook Chinese food?'*

Yes, we did our homework – *'Did you do your homework?'*

It's on the *desk* – *'Where is it?'*

Yes, he likes playing basketball – *'Does he like playing basketball?'*

She swims twice a week – *'How often does she swim?'*

It's four o'clock – *'What time is it?'*

Yes, she can ride a bike – *'Can she ride a bike?'*

I am a *teacher* – *'What do you do?'*

She is from *Britain* – *'Where is she from?'*

His name is *John* – *'What is his name?'*

They are eight years' old – *'How old are they?'*

Whose

It's *her mobile* – *'Whose mobile is it?'*

It's *our house* – *'Whose house is it?'*

The dog used to be *ours* – *'Whose dog did it use to be?'*

It *will be* their picture when I die – *'Whose house will it be?'*

It has been *her* house since 2001 – *'Whose house has it been since 2001?'*

Weather

The weather is warm and sunny *today* – *'What is the weather like today?'*

It will be stormy *tomorrow* – *'What will the weather be like tomorrow?'*

There was a lot of fog *yesterday* – *'What was the weather like yesterday?'*

It *used to be* cold and rainy here but now it is hotter – *'What did the weather use to be like?'*

Distance

It's 400 km from Madrid to Barcelona – *'How far is it from Madrid to Barcelona?'*

It was 40 km to New York – *'How far was it to New York?'*

You take the M25 to get to Brighton – *'How do you get to Brighton?'*

Los Angeles is five hours from New York by plane – *'How far is Los Angeles from New York by plane?'*

How much, how many

Next week we will have two cars – *'How many cars will you have next week?'*

He *used to* have *three houses* – *'How many houses did he used to have?'*

She does a lot of paperwork every week – *'How much paperwork does she do every week?'*

He is going to work 60 hours this week – *'How much work is he going to do this week?' 'How many hours is he going to work this week?'*

Frequency

He does karate five times a week – *'How often does he do karate?'*

She used to make an appearance every couple of months – *'How often did she used to make an appearance?'*

I would cycle to work three times a week if it didn't rain so much– *'How often would you cycle to work if it didn't rain so much?'*

He plays football every weekend he can – *'How often does he play football?'*

Measurements / degree

The table is 1.2 meters wide – *'How wide is the table?'*

An elephant weights about 4500kg – *'How much does she weigh?'*

My house is very small – *'How small is your house?'*

It's very foggy outside – *'How foggy is it outside?'*

When it is finished, the building will be 50 meters tall – *'How tall will the building be?'*

If he didn't exercise we would weigh over 200 pounds – *'how much would be weigh if he didn't exercise?'*

There used to be many blue whales in the ocean – *'How many blue whales did there used to be in the ocean?'*

But humans eat too much fish – *'How much fish to humans eat?'*

Take and last

It takes her a day to write a decent essay – *'How long does it take her to write a decent essay?'*

It took use three hours to reach a decision – *'How long did it take you to reach a decision?'*

The tennis match should last 2 hours as long as it doesn't rain– *'How long should the tennis match last?'*

It used to take me two hours to learn something new – *'How long did it use to take you to learn something new?'*

The last train journey they did lasted 50 minutes – *'How long did the last train journey you did last?'*

It would take me 20 minutes to fry this fish if we had some gas – *'How long would it take you to fly that fish if we had some gas?'*

It had taken him two hours to get the baby to sleep before you arrived – *'How long had it taken him to get the baby to sleep before you arrived?'*

This exercise has lasted 5 minutes – *'How long has this exercise lasted?'*

Still, yet, already and anymore

Yes, she has already spoken to the neighbour – *'Has she spoken to the neighbour yet?'*

Yes, he is still taking French classes – *'Is he still taking French classes?'*

No, the lake hasn't frozen yet – *'Has the lake frozen yet?'*

No, she doesn't work for them anymore – *'Is she still working for them?'*

Present perfect/present perfect continuous

I have been living in this neighbourhood for 10 years – *'How long have you been living in this neighbourhood for?'*

He has known them since he was young – *'How long has he known them for?'*

I have been making dinner – *'What have you been doing?'*

She has been wrapping presents all day – *'How long has she been wrapping presents for?'*

They have played the piano since they were at school – *'How long have they played the piano for?'*

She has had those glasses since yesterday – *'How long has she had these glasses for?'*

We have been writing the book for 3 years – *'How long have you been writing the book for?'*

To be, look, taste, smell and sound like

He has a beard and blond hair – *'What does he look like?'*

My bike is old and red – *'What does your bike look like?'*

They are argumentative but funny – *'What are they like?'*

It smells like home cooking food – *'What does it smell like?*

,

The hotel is relaxing but a bit boring – *'What is the hotel like?'*

He is like *his father* – *'Who is he like?'*

She looks like *her sister* – *'Who does she look like?'*

It sounds like rock music – *'What does it sound like?'*

It tastes sweet – *'What does it taste like?'*

Prepositions at the end of the sentence

We are responsible for this animal – *'What are we responsible for?'*

They are sailing to America – *'Where are they sailing to?'*

He was speaking to his boss – *'Who was he speaking to?'*

I am looking at your – *'Who are you looking at?'*

It's made of flour and egg – *'What is it made of?'*

They were joking about the class – *What were they joking about?*

I went to the park *with my dog* – *'Who did you go to the park with?'*

He used to dream of starting his own business – *'What did he used to dream of?'*

It was painted by *Picasso* – *'Who was it painted by?'*

He is in charge of *production* – *'What is he in charge of?'*

She used to be scared of flying – *'What did she used to be scared of?'*

If I practice every day I will be good at French – *'If you practice every day what will you be good at?'*

He is getting married to Rachel– *'Who is he getting married to?'*

They will laugh at my new sofa – *'What will they laugh at?'*

To get the right answer, you must divide by 6 – *'To get the right answer, what must you divide by?'*

7. Difficult points to teach online

Object and possessive pronouns and possessive adjectives

Level: Beginner

Object and possessive pronouns and possessive adjectives (see below) are notoriously difficult to teach as they look very similar, and can leave students confused even after weeks of practice. For this reason, in a physical class I teach them with a 'real world' application; a card game.

The card game isn't possible online and so I have recreated the idea on the Pronoun worksheet on page 91 to display on your shared screen. The object of the game is to distribute presents between the teacher, the class and other characters on the sheet. The worksheet must be downloaded in Word format so that you, the teacher, can 'move' the presents next to the characters.

Subject pronoun	Possessive adjective	Object pronoun	Possessive pronouns
I	My	Me	Mine
You	Your	You	Yours
He	His	Him	His
She	Her	Her	Hers
It	Its	It	Its
We	Our	Us	Ours
You	Your	You	Yours
They	Their	Them	Theirs

The game

Share this table found on the Pronouns worksheet on page 90 on your shared screen.

In a group lesson, Student A tells the teacher to distribute the presents using the object pronouns 'me', 'you,' 'him', 'her' and so on with the phrase 'give <u>him</u> a card' or 'give <u>her</u> a present'. Use the student box for 'give me a present', the teacher box is for 'give you...', the boy for 'give him..,' the girl for; 'give her' and the class; 'give us'. This activity should be done quickly.

Next direct your students to ask each other about the presents using as many possessive adjectives as possible. For example:

Teacher: Stuart, ask Sarah about the boy's present.

Tom: 'What is <u>his</u> present?'

Sarah: '<u>His</u> present is a dog.'

Teacher: 'Sarah, ask Lara about the class's present.'

Sarah: 'What is <u>our</u> present?'

José: 'Our present is a hat.'

When they have finished, move the presents back into the box and pick another student to direct you.

This time pick up a character's present and ask 'what is <u>her</u> present?' Elicit '<u>her</u> present is a horse' (for example) and write in the group messages: '<u>Her</u> card is a horse' or 'the horse card is <u>hers</u>.'

Underline 'hers' and elicit or explain the meaning; it is the possessive pronoun which substitutes the noun ('the horse card is <u>hers</u>' or 'The horse card is the girl'<u>s</u>'). Elicit or explain the structure and that the possessive pronoun never precedes a noun.

Direct your students to ask each other about their presents, using the questions, 'what is your, his, her, our and their present?' Get them to answer using both the possessive adjective ('<u>his</u> present is a bike') and the possessive pronoun ('the bike present is <u>his</u>.')

In a one-on-one lesson ask the student to direct you with 'give him', 'give her' and so on while you move the presents. Then ask your student to describe who has which present with possessive adjectives and pronouns.

Don't expect students to use pronouns perfectly after one lesson. This activity should be repeated several times during the term to practice.

Prepositions of place

Level: Beginner

Prepositions of place are: On, in, in front of, behind, next to, under, between and where.

In the physical classroom, I would teach prepositions of place by placing objects on a table in various positions. For example, a pen might be <u>under</u> a magazine or a cup <u>between</u> a book and a baseball cap. I would then elicit the position of the objects in relation to each other. This isn't possible online and so the teacher must use an image.

Display the Prepositions of Place image found on page 89 on your shared screen and elicit the placement of different objects. Prepositions of place are one of the first things students learn, so begin in an easy way by giving a student two options rather than a straight question. For example, 'Is the trainer next to the table or below the table?' or 'Is the blanket above the sofa or on the sofa?

Once your student is used to this go on to harder questions such as, 'where is the pen?' or 'ask me where the pen is.' For example:

Teacher: Where is the alarm clock?

Student: The alarm clock is under the sofa.

Teacher: Is the mirror next to the tall lamp or in front of the tall lamp?

Prepositions of place take time to learn. Do this practice every few weeks until perfect.

Movement verbs

Level: Lower intermediate to upper intermediate, (depending on the vocabulary)

Movement verbs are also difficult to teach online because you cannot demonstrate them as you would in a classroom. For this reason, The Ultimate Teaching ESL Online Manual offers two pages of pictures showing different movements. In addition, you'll find all the different types of 'falls', (these are: fall in, fall on, fall out, fall off, fall over and to drop), for when you're teaching fall phrasal verbs.

General vocabulary

Online, you can't draw what you mean on a blackboard and so it is important to build up a picture library to allow you to show what you are talking about on your shared screen.

Useful pictures for this include the Fruit and Vegetables, Movements, Pronouns, Prepositions of Place and Appearance worksheets

Conditionals

Level: Upper intermediate

Conditionals express a probable future, hypothetical present or impossible past depending on whether it is the first, second or third conditional respectively. They are usually used with an 'if' clause. For example, 'if it is not raining, he will take the dog for a walk,' (first conditional) or 'if you didn't smoke so much, you would feel healthier' (second conditional) or 'if she hadn't gone to the library that morning, she would never have met her boyfriend' (third conditional).

I have included conditionals in this list because they are a tough subject. You can teach conditionals just as effectively online as you would in a physical classroom by using drills. There is an example of a second conditional drill on page 38. With a little thought, you can adapt this drill to the first and third conditional. Or you can find specially designed drills, along with speaking practices, in our original book, The Ultimate ESL Teaching Manual.

Freer speaking practice: Conditionals chain story

This works with all conditionals. The teacher starts the story with the first clause of a conditional sentence, for example, 'If I had a dog...' Now ask the student to complete the sentence – for example, 'If I had a dog, I would teach it tricks.' Using the end of the last conditional sentence, create a new line.

For example, 'If I taught my dog tricks, we could join the circus.' Ask your next student to do the same using the end of this sentence. Continue like this until the story becomes boring or ceases to make sense. Then start another chain story with a new sentence.

Present continuous

The present continuous is 'to be' verb plus verb in gerund. For example, 'She is working right now.' To practice, display the present continuous worksheet on page 137 on your shared screen. Next ask your students to use the continuous form to describe what they can see in these pictures. This activity has a certain technique to it, so practice with someone before the lesson. If done right, it should start easy and then get progressively harder.

First ask questions your students can't get wrong. You do this by giving them two options, one of which is ridiculous, for example for picture A, 'is Mr Smith holding an umbrella or a cat?' Your student will automatically answer, 'he is holding a cat.' Do this a few times until they are comfortable with the complete 'he is' or 'she is' answer and then start throwing curve balls. For example:

Teacher: 'Is Mr Smith wearing a hat or a banana?'

John: 'He is wearing a hat.'

Teacher: 'And you, John?'

Instead of repeating what you say the question forces John to think and use the grammar himself to form the sentence 'I am wearing...'

Here are some suggested questions for the first two pictures to give you some ideas.

Picture one: People waiting at a train station

o   Is the boy holding flowers or a hat?
o   Is he standing or sitting? And you?
o   Is he wearing trousers or a dress? And the girl in the picture?
o   What is he looking at? And me?
o   Is the woman touching her leg or her bag?
o   Is the train moving or is it still?

- o What is the man in the blue jeans doing? And you? And me?
- o Where are they waiting?

Picture two: Passengers in an aeroplane

- o Is the woman in the orange dress sleeping or dancing?
- o Is she lying back or lying forward?
- o Is she wearing pink shoes or yellow shoes?
- o What colour shoes are you wearing? And your neighbour?
- o Is the man with the red jumper reading or writing?
- o What is he reading?
- o Are you reading?
- o Is he looking at you or the book?
- o What is the boy looking at? And you? And the other students?
- o What is he listening to? And me? And you?
- o What is he wearing? And your friend?
- o Is he feeling happy or serious? And me?
- o How are you feeling?
- o Is he dancing or sitting? And the class?
- o Are they flying in an aeroplane or travelling in a train?

Deduction and possibility

This is to practice 'must' for a positive deduction and 'can't' for a negative deduction and 'may' and 'might' for possibility. Display the Deduction and Possibility worksheet on page 138 and ask your students to make positive and negative deductions in present along with some possibilities. For example, for picture one:

John: The men in orange must be rescue workers.

Lara: The girl in the stretcher can't be feeling well.

For advanced students you can also practice deduction and possibility in past with 'must have', 'can't have', 'might have' and 'may have.' For example:

Stuart: There might have been an earth quake.

Sarah: It can't have been a normal day.

Yet/already

Yet and already are adverbs that state whether or not something has happened. They are usually used with the present perfect. Using the Yet and Already worksheet on page 139, make sentences about what the teenager has <u>already</u> done, hasn't done <u>yet</u> and is possibly <u>still</u> doing.

Give your student a sentence below and tell them to turn it into a question for another student. For individual classes, ask your student to make the question and then answer it themselves.

Here are some examples:

Teacher to Lara: 'Have a shower'

Tom to Sarah: 'Sarah, has she had a shower <u>yet</u>?'

Sarah: 'Yes, she has <u>already</u> had a shower.

Teacher to Sarah: 'Put clothes in the chest of drawers.'

Sarah to Stuart: 'Stuart, has she put the clothes in the chest of drawers <u>yet</u>?'

Tom: 'No, she hasn't put the clothes in the chest of drawers <u>yet</u>.'

Sentences

- o   Make the bed.
- o   Turn on her computer.
- o   Pack school bag.
- o   Set up speaker.
- o   Go outside.
- o   Put on shoes.
- o   Tie shoelaces.
- o   Wake up.

- o   Take the dog for a walk.

- o   Put her clothes in the cupboard.
- o   Tidy his desk.
- o   Do the washing.
- o   Practice the guitar.
- o   Brush hair.
- o   Take off pyjamas.
- o   Get dressed.
- o   Decorate room.

8. Starters and Finishers

The first 10 minutes of a class should be dedicated to an easy activity to ease your students into the lesson and the last five minutes to a high-energy, fun activity to leave the students upbeat and wanting more.

Starter activities

When I first started teaching online I tried to adapt warmer activities from classroom lessons to an online environment. I quickly found this didn't work. At the beginning of an online lesson, students are dealing with any connection and equipment problems and do not want the extra hassle of doing an activity on a shared screen (which may or may not work for them straight into the session).

For this reason I now start all of my classes with a simple but interesting question which takes students three to five minutes to answer. Those wishing to take an ESL exam will find this practice doubly useful because they are the sort of questions students must answer in an IELTS or Cambridge Exam.

Warmer Questions

Here are some of my favourite questions:

1# Tell me about somewhere you would like to visit in the future and why?

2# Tell me about the most impressive place you have ever been to? Why did it make such an impression on you?

3# If your house was on fire (and everyone was safe) what are the three things you would rescue from the flames and why?

4# Tell me about a book or film that has influenced your life.

5# Tell me about a historical figure you admire. Tell me about their life story.

6# Tell me about the best piece of advice you have ever received. Why was it useful for you?

7# Who has been the most influential figure in your life and why?

8# What are the most rewarding and challenging things about your work and why?

9# Make five predictions about your city for 10 years into the future.

10# What are the 'must-sees' and things to avoid for tourists who come to your city?

11# Tell me about the lives of your grandparents? What were their lives like? How were their lives different from yours?

12# What is the biggest problem in your city? What would you do about it, if you were mayor?

13# Tell me about three personal strengths and how have they helped you in your life?

14# Tell me about a life changing event which has happened to you or a friend or family member?

15#What are your top money saving tips?

Finisher activities

Finish your lesson with a fun, high-energy finishing activity. The end is not the time to teach something new, so make sure that the finisher activity is a review of the content they already know. Here are some ideas:

Irregular verbs in past and participle: Use the irregular verb sheets to ask quiz your students on the past and participle of irregular verbs.

Nations and nationalities: Using the World Maps on page 92 ask your students to name the nationalities of citizens of the countries. Choose a different continent each time.

Days and months: Ask your students to recite the days of the week and months backwards in a chain (guaranteed laughs).

The Short Answer drill: Use the short answer drill on page 33 to practice short answers (Have you eaten an apple today? <u>Yes, I have</u>).

The A-Z of...: Review the vocabulary topic you have just studied by asking your students to give you a word for each letter of the alphabet. For example, with the topic 'Medicine' 'A' could be for 'amputation', 'B' for 'bandage' and so on.

Make vs do

Display the Make vs Do table on page 114 on the shared screen and give your class a quick quiz on nouns paired with 'make vs do.' Download the table in Word as well as PDF so that you can fill it in with your students in real time.

You'll find words on the Make vs Do table. The download Word worksheet, however, is blank so that you can fill it out with your students.

In vs on quiz

Display the In vs On table on page 114 and give your class a quick quiz with nouns that go with 'in' and 'on'.

Dictate the words at random and elicit whether your students think it is 'on' or 'in'. To give the words context you have to say 'a person and a bike' (rather than simply 'bike') from which your student can imagine a person riding a bike and hopefully remember that the word is 'on'. Write the words in the table (in Word format) in real time.

Common questions: 'Why is a person <u>on</u> a bus, a boat and a plane but <u>in</u> a car?'

Answer: Well even though they are all closed spaces you can walk onto a bus, a boat and a plane meaning that they are less closed than a car – which is really just a box on wheels.

Words for the activity: You'll find words on the In vs On table on page 114. The download Word worksheet, however, is blank so that you can fill it out with your students.

Get in vs get on quiz

Test your class on their knowledge of transport and 'get' phrasal verbs. Give your students the following nouns and ask them to respond with the appropriate 'get' verbs.

<u>Note:</u> Make sure they say both the enter and exit verb such as: 'To get on and off a bus.'

The rules

To get on: To enter something you will be on, for example, 'To get on a bus.'

To get off: To exit something you were previously on ('To get off a bus.')

To get in: To enter something that you will be in ('To get into a car.')

To get out of: To exit something that you were previously in ('To get out of a car.')

To get into: To start an interest or find yourself in trouble. For example, 'She is getting into tennis.'

<u>Note:</u> You are 'in' something when it is a closed space. You are 'on' something you can move about on.

Words for the activity: You'll find words on the get in/off vs get on/out table on page 113. The download Word worksheet, however, is blank so that you can fill it out with your students.

In, on and at, Making Arrangements quiz

Display the In, on and at worksheet (on page 113) on the shared screen and complete it in real time. Tell your students to imagine that they are going to meet their friend and must select the correct preposition for the arrangement. Next dictate the below nouns at random and elicit the preposition.

Words for the activity: You'll find words on the In, on at table. The download Word worksheet, however, is blank so that you can fill it out with your students.

The rules

After they have completed this task, and got many wrong, tell the class the rules. I recommend this way round as students learn a lot from their mistakes.

At is for festivals (Christmas, Easter and so on), events (a party, concert or conference), time (2pm, lunchtime) and the outside of a location you can see in its entirety (the airport, the cinema, the entrance to the park), the weekend and night.

On is for days, (11th, Tuesday, my birthday, Christmas day), floors in a building, planets and 'on time' – meaning the exact point in time.

In is for places you can't see in their entirety (cities, countries, parks) as well as months, years and decades, seasons, morning, afternoon, evening, the future and a period of time (for example, let's meet in time for Christmas).

Group activity 'Making appointments': During the following class give your students four locations and times and ask them to select the correct preposition, starting with the phrase 'Let's meet.' For example:

Teacher: Dinner, park, night, spring

Lara: 'Let's meet <u>at</u> dinner, <u>in</u> the park, <u>at</u> night, <u>in</u> spring.

Other locations:

- o Paris, football stadium, Tuesday, March.
- o Beach, 12th, Morning, Mexico.
- o 2020, the concert, weekend, May.
- o 10th floor, morning, the future, my house.

9. Homework resources

Podcasts

I always ask my students to listen to a podcast for homework. This is because a) it provides excellent comprehension practice, b) the student can speak about it during the next class for speaking practice and c) there is no marking work to do by you.

Mistakes to avoid when choosing a podcast

Do not choose a podcast that is too long. Four to 10 minutes is the sweet spot – anything longer and your students will get confused meaning that the task will become a chore.

Do not choose a podcast which speaks unnaturally slowly or with a childish topic. Students need to get used to the normal pace of speaking and how native speakers actually use the language. OK, so granted, ESL podcasts do have to be simpler, but anything that is overly contrived is a waste of your students' time.

Do not use a website that requires flash player to play an MP3. Access to any homework material should be really, really easy or you'll find that half your students won't complete the assignment.

The best ESL podcasts
BBC 6 Minute English

Level: Lower-intermediate to upper-intermediate. **Accent**: British

This is without a doubt the best EFL podcast on the list and the one that I use time and time again. Updated weekly, *Six minute English* provides fun and interesting ESL podcasts on topics such as culture, technology, travel, business and more. They'll always include at least three new phrases to learn, and after listening, students can check their understanding with the transcript.

Podcasts in English

Level: Elementary to Intermediate. **Accent**: British

This site provides free three to five minute podcasts for English learners at beginner, intermediate and upper-intermediate levels. To practice comprehension and expand vocabulary, tell your students to listen to two podcasts a week and write a summary of what they hear. To do this effectively, they'll have to listen a few times.

One negative is that although the podcasts are free, students must pay for the premium version to read the transcript.

CNN 10

Level: Upper-intermediate-advanced. **Accent**: Northern American

CNN 10 is not a TEFL podcast, it is a real news show which condenses world news for that day down to 10 minutes. However, it provides a great way for higher-level students to practice their listening skills while keeping up with world news. The video can be accessed in the CNN app and students can read the full transcript afterwards to check their understanding.

A negative to this podcast is that it's not made for ESL and so speech can be fast.

ELLLO

Level: Elementary to Intermediate. **Accent**: Variable

Elllo provides thousands of free English video lessons and ESL podcasts on everyday English conversation. The podcasts consist of a dialogue between two people about an everyday topic. They are short and sweet but there are thousands of them and so you could ask your students to do one a day without much time commitment from them.

The best thing about ELLLO podcasts is that students can check their understanding with the transcript AND a quiz!

TED

Level: Upper intermediate to advanced. **Accent**: Variable

TED provides thousands of videos about technology, education, politics, science and culture.

In my experience, setting a TED talk for homework can be hit or miss. Sometimes I'd set a TED video and everyone would love it, and other times they'd complain that it was too long, too fast or too confusing to understand.

TED is still a great resource but when choosing a talk for homework this is my advice:

1. Choose a video which is no more than 10 minutes. You can separate talks by duration, topic and language in the talk tab.

2. Check that the speaker isn't speaking too fast and the accent isn't too thick (native speakers are best).

Another way to do this is to choose a theme such as 'business', 'finance' 'or 'crime' and ask your students to select and watch a TED video on the subject. Centre your following class around this theme and give your students 10 to 15 minutes to recount their video to their partners. This is a great way to reinforce the lesson vocabulary and engage your students with the topic.

TED ED: A much better choice!

A much better choice of listening is TED Ed. TED Ed is full of short educational videos about science, culture and history. Your students will be able to follow the listening much better because along with the speaker's voice there are animations to help tell the story.

Best of all, the videos are only five minutes long, and so it's a homework activity that everyone has time to do.

Grammar review

Viewing video lessons to either recap on the last grammar class or prepare for the next one is another highly productive homework activity.

Here are the best grammar video resources.

Engvid

ENGVID Provides bite-sized video lessons on most aspects of English grammar and lots of vocabulary points. Students can also read a transcript of the lesson and check their understanding with a quiz on their website.

Let's Talk: Youtube

You need it, you'll find it here. This Youtube channel has hundreds of videos on every aspect of the English language.

Writing

Writing is an essential skill and, as a TEFL teacher, you must set and mark writing assignments.

But what if there were a way for students to practice writing independently as well?

Well, there is.

Do you remember when you were learning French or Spanish at school and your teachers encouraged you to start corresponding with a foreign pen pal to improve your language skills?

Well, the concept still exists; and thanks to the internet, students stand a greater chance of finding pen pals who match their hobbies and interests, with several websites dedicated to the pastime.

If a few of the class take it up, it can also become an interesting weekly speaking practice as you catch up on the news from their pen friends, and as a group, correct the grammar and spelling on their next correspondence.

Popular Pen Pal sites

Pen Pal World, Global Pen Friends, Pen Pals Now.

Pronunciation

If your student has problems with pronunciation, asking them to watch pronunciation videos and practice in their own time is a worthwhile homework exercise. Here are some of the best sites to learn pronunciation and accent from:

Rachel's English. Accent: North American

Rachel's English undoubtedly provides one of the most comprehensive pronunciation resources on the web. Rachel will walk your students through all of the sounds in the English language. In addition, she has videos on the rhythm of English, elision (when speakers drop vowel sounds as they link words together in a sentence) and common idioms.

BBC Learning English Pronunciation Guide: Accent British

Teacher Jamie teaches students all the common sounds in the English language.

Part II

Worksheets

Worksheet downloads in high resolution

All these worksheets are available for download in PDF format from www.bilinguanation.com/speaking-book-worksheets.

Select 'The Ultimate Online ESL Manual Worksheets' and type your 8 digit Manual Owner Code **BMHYSPLA** into the box (all uppercase).

In addition, some worksheets can be downloaded in Word format to allow the teacher to modify them during the activity.

A few of these worksheets can also be found in The Ultimate Teaching ESL Manual. I have included them here because they are the best way to teach the language point online also.

All downloadable worksheets are in landscape format for a better display on the shared screen.

Instructions

Instructions for these worksheets are spread all around this book and so to make life easier I have put them all together in this reference sheet.

Icebreaker questions: These are a selection of getting-to-know-you questions for group or individual classes. Place the sheet on your shared screen and ask your students to choose a few that interest them. Because this is still an English lesson, the question is not complete and the students must do the work themselves to create a proper interrogative. Full instructions page 25.

Pronouns: A table showing subject, object and possessive pronouns and possessive adjectives. For more on how to teach them see page 67.

Prepositions of place: Elicit where these objects are in relation to one another using the prepositions of place 'on', 'in', 'under', 'in front of', 'behind', 'next to', 'between' and 'where'. Full instructions on page 69.

World map: This is useful for teaching comparative and superlative adjectives. Your students two countries and one adjective and ask them to make a sentence. For example:

Teacher: 'Norway, Portugal and snowy.'

John: 'Portugal is snowier than Norway.'

Teacher: And the reverse?

Sarah: Portugal is less snowy than Norway.

Layout of a house: This is for teaching household vocabulary with 'there is/are.' For example:

Lara: How many dining room chairs are there?

Stuart: There four dining room chairs.

There is/are with food and drink: This is for teaching 'there is/are' + 'a', 'some' and 'any.' Review what makes a countable and uncountable noun. Next, ask your students questions about the food in the picture. Ask your students also to each other. As the teacher you must direct this activity and prompt them with ideas. For example:

Teacher: John, ask Sarah about apples.

John: Sarah, are there any apples on the table?'

Sarah: Yes, there are some apples on the table and there is an orange.

Also ask, deliberately wrong questions to elicit the negative. For example:

Teacher: John, is there any beer on the table?

John: 'No, there isn't any beer on the table.'

Irregular verb story: Display one of the irregular verb sheets on your shared screen and tell your class to invent a chain story whereby one student says a line, the next continues and so on. The story must include all of these verbs in a past tense and each verb can only be used once. Full instructions page 54

Opinion and connector phrases: These are useful conversational phrases to use in debates and roleplays. Display the worksheet on your shared screen and ask your students to select one or two from a few categories to practice. Each time a student successfully includes a phrase into a sentence, they receive a point. The student with the most points in the end wins. Full instructions page 49.

Individual Roleplays: Thirteen short role plays and speaking activities to practice with your student in one-on -one classes.

Group Roleplays: A selection of sixroleplays to practice various language points. for full instructions see page 44.

In vs on vs at/ get in vs get on/ In vs on: Practice prepositions and get for transport with a pop quiz. The teacher says the noun and the students have to answer which preposition to use. Full instructions on page 77.

General debate questions: This is a set of open debate questions for speaking practice using connectors.

Prefixes and suffixes: Give your students a root word such as 'taste' or 'occupy' and your students must use as many prefixes and/or suffixes with as many words as possible in two minutes. The winner is the student who can make the most words. Afterwards, explore the meanings of the most interesting words mean and ask your students to make example sentences. A list of root words will be found on page 59.

Everyday objects: Ask your student to name these twenty everyday objects to improve their vocabulary. Which ones do they use in their life and how often?

Use the pictures to brainstorm vocabulary about household objects, chores, technology, stationary and DIY.

What will the future hold? These are images designed to provoke conversations in future tense. You can use them for 'will'; ('I think in 50 years robots will work in offices'), 'going to'; (Yes, but I don't think there is going to be a nuclear war') and present perfect future; ('By 2025 I think we will have solved the energy crisis'). <u>Remember</u>: practice each verb tense in its own dedicated class.

Starter questions: What jobs will we do in the future? Where will we live? Will we still drive? What will we eat? What big projects will the human race have accomplished by the next century?

What did the past use to be like? These images are designed to provoke conversations using 'used to'. Get your students to ask each other questions about their own countries. For example, '100 years ago did most people use to work in the country or in the city?'

Starter questions: What did your school use to be like? Did you use to wear a uniform? What technology did we use to use 20-30 years ago? What fashions did we use to have? How did families use to spend time together? How do they usually spend time together now?

Get used to These are images designed to provoke conversations using 'to be used to' and 'get used to'. For example, 'Have your parents got used to Internet shopping?' 'Yes, they are slowly getting used to it.'

Starter questions: What is your routine? When did you get used to it? Where do you live? Are you used to living there? Are you used to housing prices? Could you get used to it? What new technologies could you get used to? What couldn't you get used to?

Beach vs hiking holiday and leisure vs work: these worksheets are designed to practice comparative adjectives (for example 'the country is quieter than the city') and the quantifiers so, so much, so many, so few and so little such, too, too much, to many, too few, too little. For example, 'I prefer the city because there are too few facilities in the country.'

Other ways to use picture cards: You can find more ideas about how to use picture worksheets in the 'Describe a photo' section on page 52.

Cookery: These pictures are to teach cookery verbs and kitchen vocabulary. Elicit the vocabulary to describe each picture. In addition, get your students to ask each other questions, for example 'what is he pouring in the cup? Or 'What is she slicing?' You can also select a few photos to use as a starting point for a story.

Words: To boil, hob, oven, to squeeze, to pour, cup, kettle, to peal, banana peel, to fry, frying pan, spatula, to roll, rolling pin, dough, to slice, cut, chop, chopping board, knife, to stir, pot.

Medicine: These pictures are designed to teach medicine vocabulary.

Words: To cough, a cough, to sneeze, a cold, the flu, to have a headache, pain-killer, to have a temperature, to sweat, to feel dizzy, to have toothache, to swell, to be swollen, to break a bone, to twist, to put in plaster, plaster cast, sling, to vomit, to be sick, to feel sick to feel nauseous, tissue, to have a rash, to itch, to scratch.

Movements: These images are for movement vocabulary.

Words: To squat, to lie down, to sit up, to stretch, to skip, to lift, to bend, to bend over, to bend down, to reach to shoot to aim, to step, to step on, to tread on.

To fall: These are photos to teach the phrasal verbs 'to fall over', 'to fall in', 'to fall down', 'to fall off', 'to fall out' and 'to drop'. Elicit each type of fall and explain the difference.

Next check your student's understanding with this quiz. The teacher says a noun from the list below and the student must decide which 'fall' it is. For example:

Teacher: 'A tooth from a mouth.'

Tom: 'A tooth <u>falls out</u> of your mouth.'

Make sure you select the 'falls' at random.

To fall in: A fly into soup, with bad people, a swimming pool, a well.

To fall out: From a train, from a bus, a euro from my pocket, from a tree, hair, tooth from a mouth, a person from a window.

To fall off: From a boat, from a branch, a person from the top of a building, a hat from a head, a child from a swing, a lamp from a table, a person from a cliff, a person from a ladder, a person from a balcony.

To fall over: A lamp on the floor, a person in the street, a shopping trolley/cart.

To fall down: A person from a mountain, a person from a well (also fall in), a person from stairs, a person from a hill.

To drop: An umbrella from my hand, a person in the street, keys from my person, a bone from a dog.

Just/ just about to: These images are designed to teach the adverb 'just' with present perfect and the phrase 'just about + infinitive'. Ask your students to identify what they think has just happened and what they think is just about to happen.

Facial appearance

Teach facial vocabulary with these pictures.

Suggested vocabulary: To wear glasses, to have a beard, moustache, red, brown, blond hair, long, short hair, curly, straight, wavy hair, clean-shaven.

Appearance and personality: This image is designed to teach clothing, appearance and personality vocabulary, together with the questions 'what does he/she look like?' and 'what do you think he/she is like?

Follow on questions:

- o   What their brothers / sisters look like.
- o   Whether they and their siblings look alike.
- o   Whether they look like their father or mother.
- o   What they used to look like at school.
- o   What their house looks like.
- o   What they think they will look like in the future.

- o   Whether they are like their father or mother.
- o   What they used to be like at school.
- o   What their job / school is like.
- o   What their favourite / least favourite person is like.

Words: Coat, shirt, tie, trousers, shoes, jacket, sweater, pockets, loose, tight, to loosen, to tighten, skirt, top, high heels, watch, shorts, suit, to suit, handbag, to carry, beard, short hair, long hair, a bob, curls.

Tongue twisters: These are 10 tongue twisters for your students to try.

Present continuous: Ask your students to describe what's happening in these photos using the present continuous. Full instructions on page 71.

Deduction and possibility: Ask your students to make positive and negative deductions with 'must' and 'can't' and possibility statements possibility with 'may' and 'might' about what is happening in these pictures. Full instructions on page 72.

Yet and already: Using 'yet' and 'already' make questions and answers about what the teenager has already done and what she hasn't done yet. Full instructions on page 73.

Reflexive pronouns: Using the reflexive pronoun; myself, yourself, himself, herself and so on and the phrase 'each other' (which signifies interaction with someone else) ask your students to describe what is happening in these pictures.

Had better: Your students must repair a house. Using 'had better' tell them to decide which jobs they can do and which they have to leave for a professional. For example, 'We had better fix the roof before it rains.

Icebreaker questions

What/ name?

Where/ live?

Where/ mother/ from?

What / do? (profession)

How old / house?

Where/born?

What time/ where you live? (indirect question)

What / weather / today?

What / favourite/ _____?

What TV show/ watching right now?

What / boss's, brother's, sister's, friend's, pet's/ name?

How often/play sport? And your brother/sister?

Where/neighbour buy fruit and vegetables?

When/ last time / drive?

When / last time / cook?

How / cook / favourite dish?

Have you ever / be to _____?

How often / national holidays / your country?

How long / learn English?

/completed homework yet?

What/ do / last weekend?

What year / father born?

When / last time / speak English

How long / take / get ready in the morning?

How hot/ outside?

How much fruit/ eat a week?

How / average giraffe weigh?

/know how/ swim?

Have/had breakfast yet?

/tell apart Coke from Pepsi?

How/ things / know about Vikings?

How far / supermarket/ your house?

/ tell apart the words anger and hunger?

How/ things/know about Romans?

What/want to be/ when/ growing up? And your siblings?

What/ most difficult thing/ English for you?

How long/ learning English for?

What / thinking/ before/ lesson?

Tell me about/interesting thing/ happen last week. (indirect question)

What/ your house look like?

What / people outside / doing?

When / humankind / go back / moon?

/ used to have / pet / when/ growing up?

/ used to play an instrument when/ younger?

Would/ever/ emigrate? Where to?

Would/ ever start/ own business? What?

When /last time/ laugh? Why?

What/ want to have achieved/ by the time/ turn 70? And your family?

How long/ last film/ watch/ last?

Any questions for me?

Prepositions of place

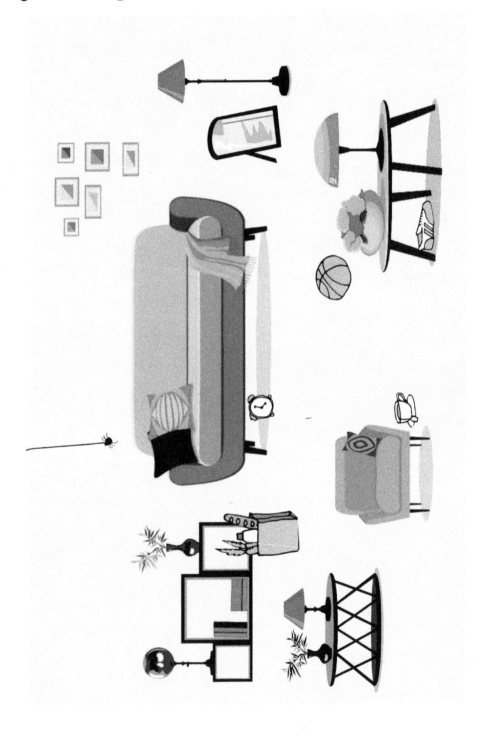

Pronouns

Subject pronoun	Object pronoun	Possessive adjective	Possessive pronouns
I	Me	My	Mine
You	You	Your	Yours
He	Him	His	His
She	Her	Her	Hers
It	It	Its	Its
We	Us	Our	Ours
You	You	Your	Yours
They	Them	Their	Theirs

Object and possessive pronouns and possessive adjectives

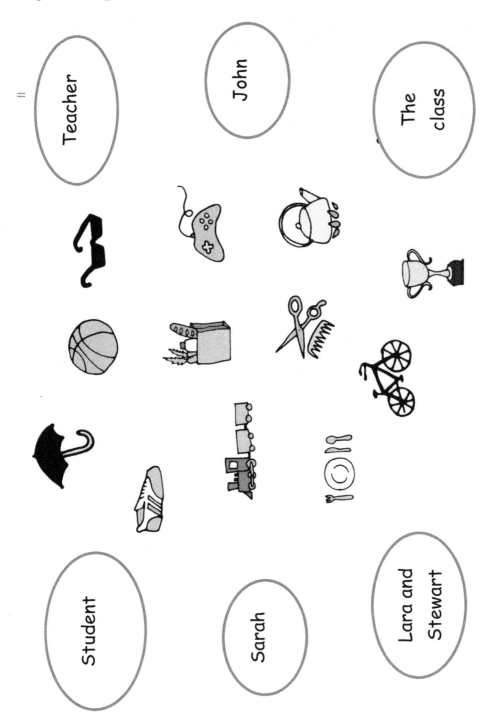

Map: Europe and Africa

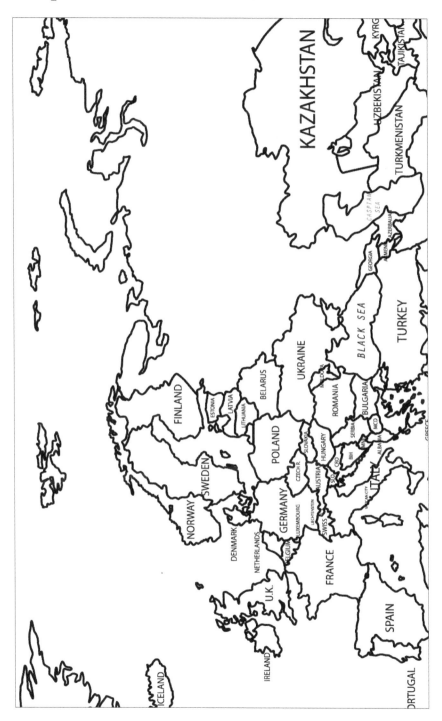

The Americas

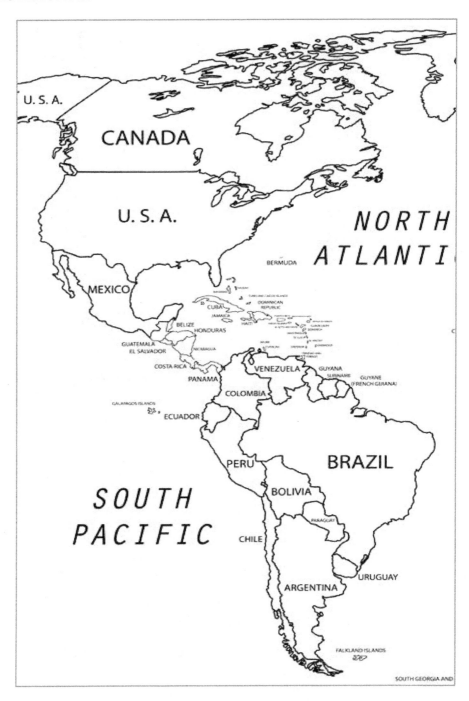

South East Asia and Oceania

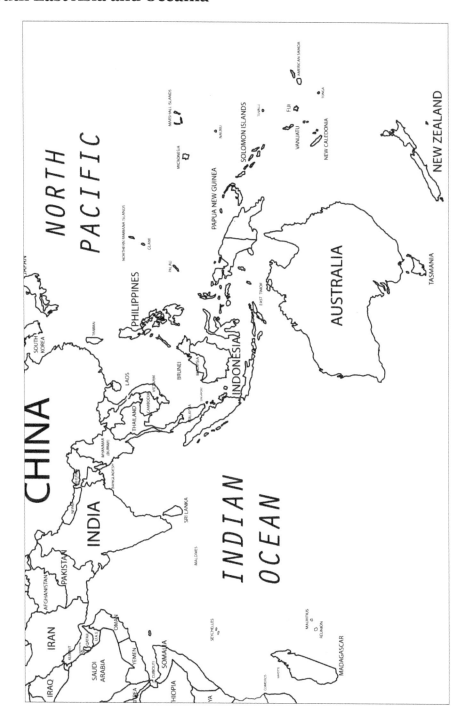

Layout of a house

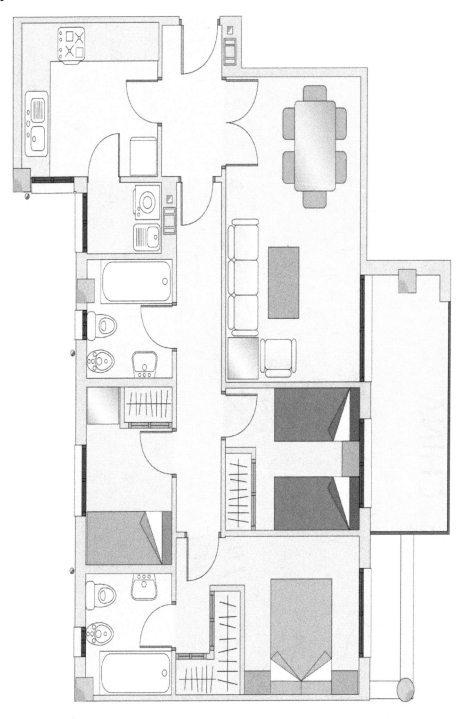

There is/there are some and any

Irregular verb story I

Run	Say	Begin	Catch	Buy
Drive	Hear	Make	Think	Fall
Choose	See	Pay	Sleep	Read
Bring	Put	Eat	Know	Send
Break	Come	Fight	Do	Give

Irregular verbs story II

Sit	Grow	Keep	Fly	Get
Throw	Win	Leave	Drink	Speak
Wear	Find	Spend	Feel	Come
Cut	Have	Take	Hold	Go
Lose	Meet	Become	Sell	Choose

Irregular verbs advanced I

Hang	Ring	Forbid	Spill	Bite
Freeze	Sink	Spend	Draw	Teach
Quit	Shave	Bleed	Bend	Show
Lend	Swear	Rise	Blow	Sweep
Shine	Mislead	Fight	Mean	Hear

Irregular verbs advanced II

Sting	Swim	Sow	Ride	Dig
Forgive	Bear	Shine	Under-stand	Tear
Deal	Creep	Wind	Stand	Feed
Lay	Shake	Light	Speed	Spin
Shoot	Seek	Slide	Shrink	Misun-derstand

Connectors and phrases I

1 Opinions	2 And	3 But
a) In my opinion b) I think c) I believe d) I am in favour of I reckon	a) In addition to b) As well as c) Along with d) Furthermore Moreover	a) However b) Apart from c) Nevertheless d) Despite + gerund e) In spite of + gerund f) On the contrar g) Although + indica- tive
5 Explaining your reasons	**6 Agreeing/ Disagreeing**	**7 Structuring**
a) Due to + noun b) Due to the fact that + verb c) Since / as + verb d) Thanks to + noun e) Therefore + verb f) In case + verb	a) To agree/ disagree b) You're right c) To come to an agreement d) Let's compromise	a) Firstly b) Secondly c) Finally d) First of all... A, b, c...
4 Consequence	**8 Conclusions**	
a) So b) So that c) Because d) In case e) Consequently f) Therefore g) Which means that	a) To sum up b) To conclude c) In short d) In summary e) Above all Overall	

Connectors and phrases II

7.Your honest opinion	8.Expressing how the situation affects you	9. Referencing a source
a) Frankly b) Truthfully c) To be honest d) To tell the truth	a) Personally speaking b) As far as I'm concerned c) From my point of view	a) According to b) Regarding, concerning c) In relation to d) For example e) In fact f) Namely
11 When you're not sure of the facts a) They say that b) From the look of things c) For some d) It is understood that... e) As far as I know In theory	**12 Uncertainty** a) I am not sure/certain b) Supposedly c) It's on the tip of my tongue d) As far as I know e) It depends on	**13 . Exclamations** a) No doubt about it b) Never again c) You're right d) I swear to you e) No way! f) You're joking! g) You're kidding h) Absolutely!
10. Giving examples a) Especially b) Particularly c) Specifically d) Let me give you an example	**14 Clarifying** a) In what sense? b) What do you mean? c) To what extent?	

Quick roleplays for individual classes

Modal verbs for obligation and prohibition

Must, should, mustn't, shouldn't and have to/ don't have to (which are not modal verbs).

The teacher is a visitor to the student's city. The student must advise the teacher about where to go and what to do, see, try, eat, drink and so on using obligation and prohibition verbs.

For example: 'You must visit the monument in the town square.' 'You shouldn't hire a car, there is nowhere to park.'

Modal verbs for deduction and possibility

Must, can't, may and might.

Use the deduction and possibility pictures and ask your student to create sentences like, 'she must be a teacher,' and 'she can't be having a good time.'

Future tenses

Will, going to and present continuous for future plans.

Ask the student to tell you about their future holiday plans. Include things that they are going to do for certain and things they will do if the weather is good or if they have time.

Past simple

Ask the student to recount a past holiday. Alternatively, ask the student to watch a five minute TED Ed animation about a historical figure or event and tell them to explain it to you the next lesson. This is also a good way to use 'used to.'

For example, 'The Romans used to speak Latin.'

'Used to' for past

Ask your student to name a retired sports star who you have both heard of. The teacher then plays the part of the sports star and the student interviews them using 'used to' plus different interrogative pronouns.

For example, if the teacher is Michael Jordon the student may ask, 'how often did you use to practice?' 'How many matches did you use to play a month?' 'What did you use to wear?' 'How car did you use to run?'

To be used to/ to get used to + gerund

Both the student and teacher have started new jobs and must interview each other about what they are used to and what they are getting used to. Choose interesting jobs to improve the conversation. My preferred job is a long-distance truck driver in the USA.

Questions include: 'Are you used to waking up early?' 'When did you get used to being alone for most of the week?' 'Have you got used to driving long distances?'

Verbs followed by a gerund and infinitive

For example, 'to like', 'to love', 'to hate', 'to not mind', 'to start', 'to stop', 'to begin', 'to finish' (gerund) and 'to want', 'to need', 'to try', 'to decide', 'to plan', 'would like' (infinitive)

The student is a careers counsellor and must interview the teacher on their invented likes and dislikes to find the perfect career for them.

For example, 'do you like being inside or outside?' 'Do you mind travelling long distances to work?' 'Would you like to work with animals?

Get + adjective

To get tired, hungry, angry, sleepy, worried, bored, wet, thirsty, anxious, worse, better and so on.

The student is a doctor and must help the teacher solve a problem by asking lots of 'to get' + adjective questions. Favourite problems include, 'I can't sleep' and 'I can't stop eating.'

Questions your student may ask could be, 'how often do you get hungry at night?' 'When was the last time you got anxious?' 'How long does it take you to get sleepy in the evening?' 'Do you get thirsty at night?' 'Is the problem getting worse or better?'

So, so much, so many, so few, so little

Ask your student to name you a place they don't want to visit. The teacher then plays the role of a travel agent from hell. It is the teacher's your job to persuade the student to buy a holiday to this destination while the student must object using 'so', 'so much', 'so many' and 'so few'.

Destinations that I use are Siberia and the Sahara Dessert. For example, there is so much snow/sand.' 'It's so hot or cold.' 'There are so many mosquitos/bears.'

Too, too much, too many, enough

I actually use 'The travel agent from hell' roleplay for this language point also. However, for some variation you could change it to 'The salesperson from hell.' For this, ask your student to name a vehicle that they would never buy. The teacher must try to sell the vehicle while the student must object using 'too', 'too much', 'too many' and 'enough'.

For example, if the vehicle was a tractor, objections could include 'it's too slow'; 'it uses too much petrol'; 'there are not enough seats' and so on.

Passive voice: Object + to be + participle

The student is the boss and you are the bad employee. The student must ask the teacher to do things around the office using passive voice so as not to offend them. For example, rather than 'you must clean the kitchen', a student would say, 'the kitchen must be cleaned.'

Jobs include: Send a report, write an email, organise a meeting, fix the photocopier, complete a project.

Passive voice with 'to get': Object + to be + to get

The student must separate themselves from something bad that they did by using the passive voice. For this, the student is a captain and the teacher a farmer. During an army exercise, the captain and his companions accidentally destroyed a house in a rural area. No one was injured but the captain must explain the incident to the farmer.

Sentences could include: 'Your farm house got destroyed', 'you will get paid compensation', no one got hurt', and 'some sheep got killed.'

Second conditional

The student and teacher take it in turns to ask 'If' questions. For example, 'if you could be a superhero, what power would you choose?' 'If you found 10,000 euros in your bank account, what would you do with it?' 'If you could eliminate one character from the Star Wars franchise, who would it be and why?' 'If you wrote a best-selling novel, what would it be about?'

Unless, as long as, provided that and even if

Ask your student about a typical work or home life situation. You take on the part of the boss who wants something done by a certain time and the student must negotiate the tasks and deadline using these conditional phrases.

For example, 'we couldn't complete the project by that time unless you gave us more staff.'

Six roleplays for group classes

Roleplay one: The theme park mascot

Warmer questions

- o What's the worst low-paid job you or a friend/family member has ever had?
- o What made it so bad?
- o Have you ever seen a theme park mascot? What do you think their work day is like?
- o What are the problems with being a theme park mascot?
- o What are the advantages?

Roleplay

Young worker: You are spending your summer working as a theme park mascot but you want to switch to a job in the park's fast food restaurant. Why did you take this job? And why do you want to change?

Manager: You would prefer the young worker to remain a mascot for the rest of the summer. Do you like the young worker? Why/Why not? Why are you refusing to let him/her change jobs?

Human resources manager: You hired the young worker and support the change of roles, but the decision rests with the manager. Why did you hire the young worker? What can you do to influence the situation?

Fast food restaurant worker: If the young worker takes a job in the restaurant, you have to be the mascot. How do you feel about this? Why are you working in the theme park?

Two-person version: The same situation but using only the young worker and manager.

Roleplay two: The Erasmus Student from Hell

- o Have you ever had a difficult flatmate? Can you tell us some stories?
- o What is the Erasmus scheme? What are the advantages of studying abroad?
- o What are the disadvantages?
- o Do you know anyone who has been an Erasmus student?
- o If you could study abroad, where would you like to study?

Students: You are two/three Erasmus students studying in [insert name of city]. After many years together neither of you want to live together anymore. You both think that the other is anti-social and has bad habits. Your flatmate did something very annoying the previous year; explain it to them using 'wish.'

Landlord: You don't want to lose your tenants. Try to help them reconcile.

Two person version: The same roleplay with two students.

Roleplay three: The press conference

Warmer questions: use picture sheet What will the future hold I? on page 118 to help develop some ideas.

- o What are the most serious problems facing mega-cities like London, New York, Hong Kong in the 21st century?
- o Would you ever live in a city like this? Why/why not?
- o What are the major problems in your city/province right now (e.g. pollution, transport, housing, crime)?
- o With climate change/population changes, what problems do you think your city or province will have in 20 years' time? What would you do about them if you were the mayor?

Roleplay

It is the year [insert] and your city is facing the serious problems of [insert problems]. The people call a press conference with the mayor to discuss how these issues are impacting on their lives and how the government plans to solve them.

Mayor: You are in charge of the city. How have these problems affected the running of the city? Why can't you solve them?

Newspaper journalist: You want answers. Why has nothing been done about this? What is stopping them fixing it? What ideas do you have to improve the situation?

Small business owner: How have these problems impacted on your business? What are you personally doing to improve the situation?

Inventor: You believe you have invented a solution for the problem. What is it? How much will it cost? What are the disadvantages?

Two-person version: The same roleplay with the mayor and the journalist.

Roleplay four: Making a movie

- o What movie genres can you think of (e.g. horror, romance, action, science fiction)?
- o If you were going to make a movie which genre would you choose?
- o What job titles can you name in the movie business? (director, producer, cameraman/woman etc).
- o What facilities and locations would a film crew need to make a movie? What would make filming difficult?
- o Where, in your opinion, is the most inconvenient country to film in, because of its geography and/or government? Explain why.

The roleplay

The director: You are making a new [insert genre] film. You are looking for a place to film your movie. Two ambassadors have approached you to make it in their countries but you have doubts about what they're offering.

Ambassador one: You are the ambassador of [insert name of inconvenient country here] and you want the director to make the film in your country. You must sell your country to the director and counter any doubts he/she may have about working there.

Ambassador two: You are the ambassador of [insert name of inconvenient country here] and you want the director to make the film in your country. You must also sell your country to the director and counter any doubts he/she may have about working there.

Producer: You want the director to choose one of the ambassadors' countries because they are cheap and you want to keep costs down.

Two-person version: The same roleplay with the director and one ambassador.

Roleplay five: City planners

Warmer questions

- o Is pollution a problem where you live?
- o What could the people/local government do to reduce it?
- o Name three types of fossil fuels and three types of green energy?
- o What problems does poor air quality cause for people?
- o What can governments do to improve air quality in cities? Can you give examples of where this is happening?

Roleplay

Air quality in the city is worse than ever. For this reason, city planners are proposing making the inner city a car free zone.

Mayor: You like the idea. Answer people's questions about why you think it's a good idea.

Owner of a large department store: You, like many other business owners in the area, hate the idea. Make your argument against the change.

Resident who lives in the inner city: You are not against the idea, but you own a car and want to know the details of the proposal.

Journalist of local paper: You are for the idea but don't think it goes far enough. Why didn't the government do something about the problem years ago? What is your proposal?

Two-person variation: The same roleplay using the mayor and the business owner.

Roleplay six: Starbucks on Mars

Warmer questions

- What are the problems of allowing international chains into an area? What are the benefits?
- What would it be like to live on a colony of 6000 people? Would you enjoy it? Why/why not?
- How would you keep yourself entertained?
- What facilities would humans have to cultivate to be able to live on Mars? (A dome, a source of water, a way to grow crops etc).

Roleplay

Humans set up a colony on Mars 80 years ago and the population has grown to 6000 people. Starbucks would like to set up a coffee shop. If approved, Starbucks would be the first chain business to enter the colony.

Starbucks representative: Make a case for why your business would benefit the people of Mars.

Mayor of Mars City: You are undecided whether you are for or against the idea. You want to make the best decision based on your citizens' happiness. What questions can you ask Starbucks?

Small business owner: You are against the idea. Why?

Local resident: You are also undecided but you are curious about what Starbucks has to offer. Why?

Two-person version: The same roleplay with the Starbucks representative and small business owner.

General debate questions

1. Universities and colleges should not charge students a fee. Agree/disagree.	2. Life in my country was better 20 years ago. Agree/disagree.	3. Politicians could do more to slow climate change. Agree/disagree.
4. Robots will take most middle-class jobs in the next 30 years. Agree/disagree.	5. Tablets and mobile phones are beneficial to children. Agree/disagree.	6. Hollywood has run out of movie ideas. Agree/disagree.
7. Fashion serves no purpose. Agree/disagree.	8. Maths is the most important subject at school. Agree/disagree	9. Anyone can learn to be a great leader. Agree/disagree

What's the word? I

At	On	In
Christmas, New Year, Easter (festival). Airport, cinema (outside a building).	Tuesday, 11th, my birth-day. Ninth floor, Christmas Day. The beach New Year's Eve.	Country, city, park or plaza (open space). Inside a building. Summer.
Lunch (meals), time. House/home.	On time (the point of time). The moon.	Morning, afternoon, evening. The future, 2015, 80s. In time (the period of time).
Weekend, night, the con-cert, The conference, the party (event).		

Get in/get out	Get on/get off
A shower, a bath, a lift/elevator A rowing boat, a submarine	A bus, a bike A skateboard, a horse
	A plane, a ship or large boat
Get into: Music, spinning university	

What's the word II

In	On
A person and: water, trouble, bed (under sheets). A film, tree, bath, shape (exercise), marriage. A car, a submarine, shower, the attic. The future, June, the eighties (80s). The centre, free time. Time (within a period of time). A child playing and snow, a plane and the sky.	Person and: A bike, TV, bed (above sheets). A bus, the toilet, the telephone, the Internet. The left, the right, time (at a point of time). Fire, boat, holiday, the floor. The 15th of January, Tuesday.

Make	Do
The bed, A change, A choice, A decision, A list, A noise, A living, A mistake, A speech, An announcement, An effort, An appointment, trouble, An offer, An excuse, An impression, A pact, A reservation, A discovery, A fortune, An arrangement, A promise, A request A phone call.	A job, A favour, Business, Nothing, Something, Exercises, Homework, Better, Your best, Research, An investigation, The shopping, The dishes, The washing, Housework.

Prefixes and suffixes

Dis

Anti

Im

Extra

Pre

De

Re

Over

Semi

Post

Super

Un

Sub

Under

---

ify/fy

ness

ate

ment

ship

er/or

able/ible

acy

al

dom

ful

y

ity/iy

ist

ous/ious

_ion/tion

Everyday objects

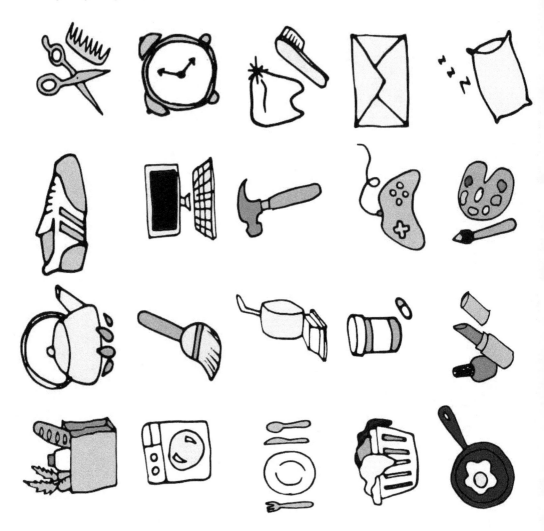

Appearance

What will the future hold? I

What will the future hold? II

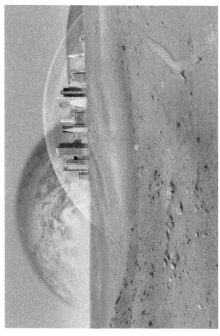 

What did the past used to be like?

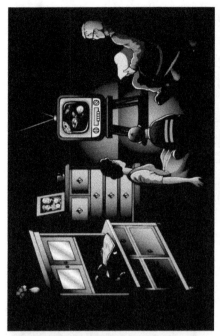

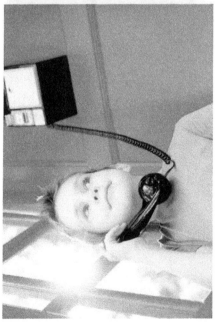

Are you used to it? Will you get used to it?

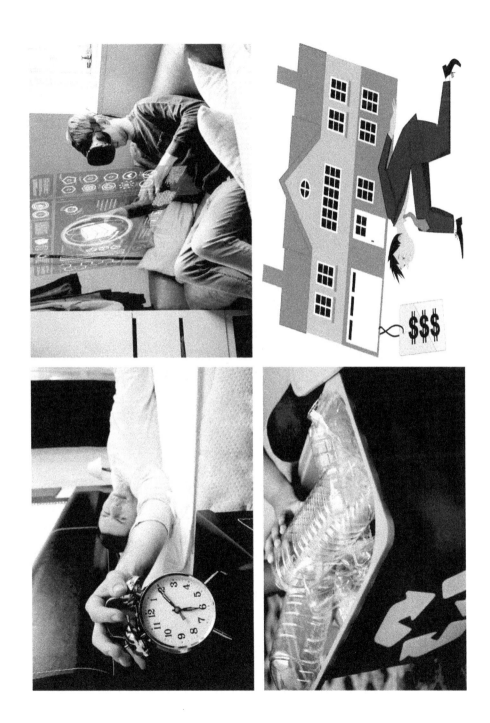

Compare and contrast

Compare and contrast

Actions: Cooking

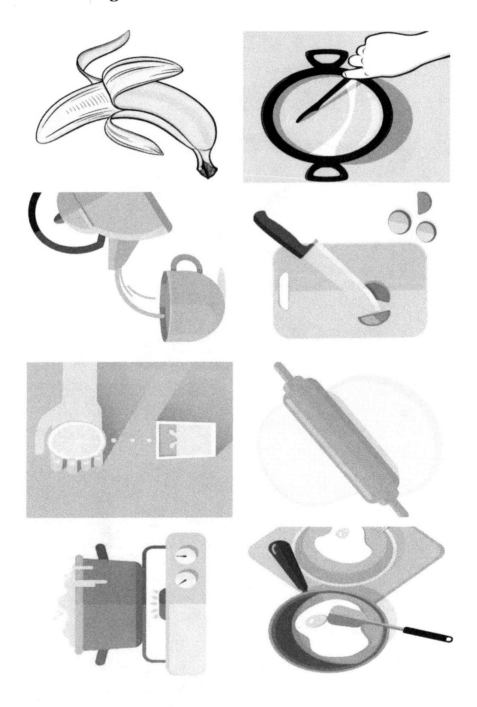

Actions: Medical problems

Actions: Body movements

Actions: To fall

Just/Just about to

Appearance and personality

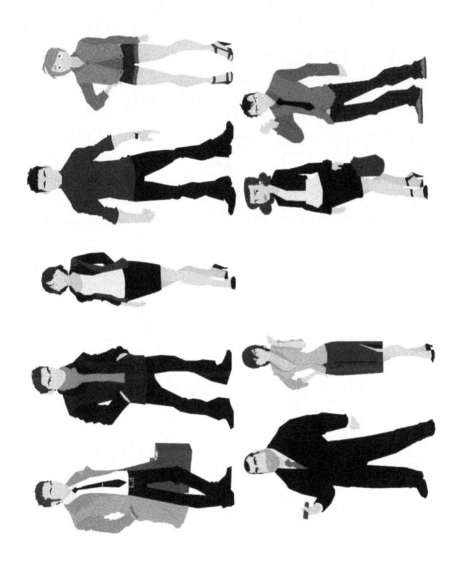

Tongue twisters

1. Though Thor thought the threat was bad, he threw the thought away.

2. What wood would you choose if it were wound in worms?

3. I saw Suzie selling sea shells on the sea shore.

4. Bertie brought bright blue berries bought aboard a boat abroad.

5. The shy shape should shop for shorts online.

6. You know you need unique New York now it's not naughty.

7. Layla lied loudly 'I love yous', lying on the luxurious leopard skin.

8. Horrible Harry had a huge hilarious horse on a hill in Huntingdon.

9. Boris's board game bored the bee badly.

10. Lucy the lawyer loved Lithuanian literature like no one else.

Present continuous

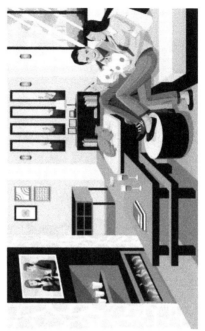

Deduction and possibility

Yet and already

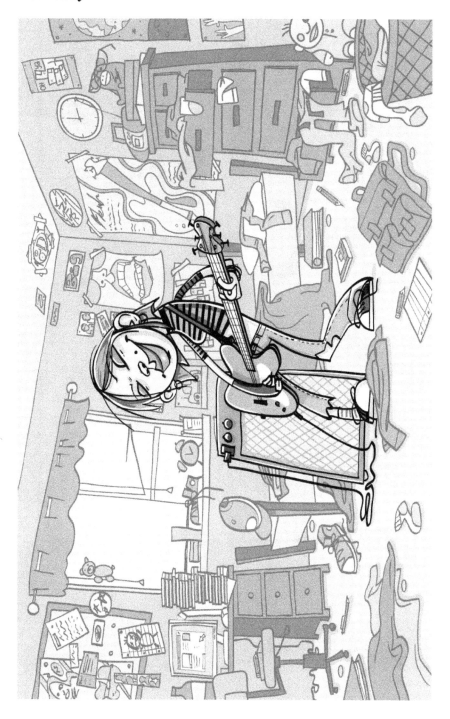

Reflexives

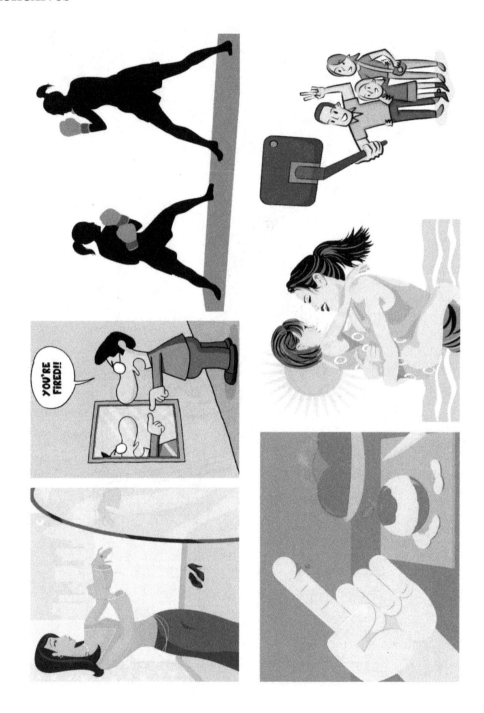

Had better

You've inherited a house!

You have just inherited a house form your great aunt. You have $10,000 to spend on the renovation. Decide what you must hire other people to do and what you can do yourselves.

- o   Fitting new windows: $3000
- o   Getting rid of rubbish: $400
- o   Fitting a new roof: $2000
- o   New drains: $800
- o   Fitting new floors: $2000
- o   Rebuilding garage: $1000
- o   Fitting new bathrooms: $2000
- o   Rewiring electricity $1000
- o   Fitting a new kitchen: $5000
- o   Building a new fireplace: $1000
- o   Gardening: $1000
- o   Fitting a new front door: $800
- o   Painting: $1000
- o   Fitting a security alarm: $1000

Additional Materials

Worksheet downloads in high resolution

To download all of these activities in colour and high resolution please visit http://www.bilinguanation.com/eslworksheets. Select the activity which you wish to download and type your 8 digit Manual Owner Code **BY6K8JUA** into the box (all uppercase).

Found this book useful?

Then check out its accompanying book The Ultimate Teaching English as a Second Language Manual.

'What a great book! Andromeda's knowledge and experience shines through. She gets straight to the point, gives very clear grammar explanations and loads of practical help' Sheila Longden, Amazon.co.uk ★ ★ ★ ★ ★

'This is a one-stop shop for preparing powerful classes that throws out the need for costly and confusing text books. Priceless!' Amazon.com Customer ★ ★ ★ ★ ★

'Great for anyone wanting to help others learn English - whether you are an ESL teacher or not!! I've been teaching for over 20 years, and this is exactly the method I have found works best.' J. Velykorodnyy, Amazon.com ★ ★ ★ ★ ★

The Ultimate ESL Teaching Manual is a complete teaching system starting from complete beginner going right up to C2-advanced level. It contains drills and speaking activities for every grammar point as well as methodology, games, vocabulary sets and a whole host of other stuff to make your classes special.

All this comes at a fraction of the price you'd spend on a collection of English language textbooks covering the same levels.

Buy now from Amazon.com for $8.85-$17.99 or Amazon.co.uk for £7.99-£12.49. Or for more information visit our website www.bilinguanation.com

Want to learn to speak Spanish?

Then check out Spanish for Geniuses: Advanced classes to get you speaking with fluency and confidence.

'This is the BEST Spanish grammar book. I own many Spanish books, what makes this one different is that she briefly explains how one would use or say the grammar point in English and then proceeds to tell you how you would say it in Spanish. Trust me this book has it all! 'Booklover, Amazon.com ★★★★★

'This is so much more useful than the usual language book formats and gives lots of help with those in-between words that help conversation flow more naturally.' Frosties, Amazon.co.uk ★★★★★

What's covered in the book

Detailed explanations on all grammar including verb tenses, nouns, adjectives, adverbs, pronouns, participles and the subjunctive as well as box-outs highlighting the differences between English and Spanish grammar and translation lists.

A comprehensive 'how do you say?' section covering phrases to use in all types of conversations including how to talk about feelings and ideas, give and receive advice, organise an event and even tell a joke.

Buy now from Amazon.com for $5.99-$12.99 or Amazon.co.uk for £3.99-£9.99.Or for more information visit our website www.bilinguanation.com

About the Author

Andromeda Jones is an ESL teacher and writer. She discovered her gift for teaching when she moved abroad and found her calling.

She is an advocate for language teaching without textbooks to enable fun dynamic classes and above all provide lots of speaking practice.

She is passionate about both teaching students and helping other teachers develop their skills to provide fantastic English classes.

She decided to put down everything she had learnt through her years of experience in a 335 page book; The Ultimate Teaching ESL Manual. This was followed by The Ultimate Teaching ESL Book of Speaking Activities and then book three; The Ultimate Teaching ESL Online Manual.

She has also written 'Spanish for Geniuses;' a comprehensive guide to Spanish.

When she is not teaching or writing she likes to spend time with her husband and children hiking in the mountains of sunny Valencia, Spain.

CPSIA information can be obtained
at www.ICGtesting.com
Printed in the USA
BVHW010226280420
578674BV00021B/124